Continuous Improvement Marketing

Other Books by the Author

LEAN ENTERPRISE LEADER
How to Get Things Done without
Doing It All Yourself

BRAND ADVERTISING
How to Create Work that Connects
with Customers Every Time

THE CEO'S GUIDE FROM GOOD TO GREAT
How to Focus the Power of Your People
and Move to the Next Level

THE MAGIC OF MISSION
Discover Your Purpose, Find Meaning,
Achieve Success, and Above All, Be Happy

DEATH IN ADVERTISING
A Whodunit

Continuous Improvement Marketing

by

Stephen Hawley Martin

WWW.OAKLEAPRESS.COM

TABLE OF CONTENTS

Part One
Continuous Improvement Marketing

Chapter One
A Bird's Eye View of Our Process

More than 2500 years ago, the Greek philosopher Heraclitus of Ephesos said, "Change is the only constant in life." He was right, of course, but I doubt he'd have been able to comprehend how quickly change happens in the twenty-first century. It's a brutal fact that if you aren't constantly transforming and evolving your business to improve what you do, how you do it, and how you communicate what you have to offer, it will not be long before you are left in the dust. Consider what has become, during the past twenty years, of once high-flying brands such as MySpace, Blockbuster, Atari, Circuit City, and Blackberry. They, along with many less known brands, have gone out of business. The point is that every organization or brand is in danger of failing and going belly up if it does not evolve at the same pace as, or preferably faster than, the culture, technology, and the market it serves. This book reveals a process my colleagues and I have developed to help our clients get out in front and stay out in front of the competition, and thereby to avoid such an unfortunate fate.

As the words of Heraclitus of Ephesos quoted above indicate, change has always been the norm. What's different today is how fast it happens. Perhaps never before in the history of humankind has so much change taken place so quickly. For example, Eli Whitney invented the cotton gin in 1793, but it wasn't until the 1830s that it started to radically increase productivity and reduce the need for human labor in cotton fields throughout the Old South.

If introduced nowadays, something like the cotton gin likely would be in widespread use within five years. To make this point, when making a presentation, I often use a widely viewed YouTube video of a 1994 Today Show episode. My audience almost always laughs, if they do not gasp, when Bryant Gumbel and Katie Couric wonder aloud what in the world this new-fangled thing is called the Internet. Yet five years later, a website on that new-fangled thing was as essential to anyone starting a company as a business card and letterhead.

It's 1994 and *Today Show* hosts, Bryant Gumbel and Katie Couric wonder, what in the world this thing is called, "Internet."

Today, a website can and should be much, much more. For starters, a website is very likely the only opportunity many businesses will have to make that all-important good first impression. Yet the potential value of a website goes much farther because the behavior of buyers has shifted so dramatically.

Today, prospective buyers consume information only when and how they want it, and perhaps more often than not, they do so without the involvement of a sales person. Prospective customers today want information, but they do not want—perhaps may even resent—being sold to. As a result, websites and new forms of inbound marketing content such as social media, podcasts, and blogging are now more important factors in the buy-sell cycle than many business people could have imagined a few years ago. That's why *Continuous Improvement Marketing* has become essential.

So how does it work? How can it put your organization and keep your organization on the cutting edge? The six-step process is one that I have developed, improved, and refined over a period of thirty years. I'll touch on each step briefly here and expand on them in the chapters that follow. It all begins with discovery.

Discover

The discovery process identifies and defines a company or brand's strengths and how well they connect or do not connect with the market. I employ primary and secondary research to conduct a thorough analysis and examine stakeholder as well as customer and prospect attitudes to see where you stand *vis a vis* the competition. From this I usually identify opportunities and challenges—things you are doing well and things that ought to be eliminated or overcome.

Develop

Existing and potential value propositions are tested with customers via focus groups, one-on-one, and with electronic surveys. Working hand and glove with a client client, this enables us to rank messages and to develop strategies to explore and consider. Each aspect of marketing is scrutinized including what the product or service offers or could offer, as well as pricing, distribution methods, and the types of promotions likely to be most effective. An action plan is the result.

Align

Effort may be required to insure your organization or brand delivers on a new or revised promise. The website may need work; modifications may be required to packaging, pricing, or decor in the case of retail. New methods of delivery may be called for; orientation or employee training might be necessary. We find that organizations thrive when their people are steeped in the brand and believe in it.

Engage

Once alignment has taken place, it's time to engage. That means rolling out communications and the engagement plan forged in the Develop stage. This may involve a push by the sales force, stepped up interaction with customers through social media, events, promotions, and traditional media— whatever has been called for. This is where many marketers begin and end their efforts, but I have found it's necessary to go further if you want the business to grow, prosper, and remain on the cutting edge.

Track

It's important to see what's working and what isn't. Google Analytics, for example, allows us to track page and visitor volume and visitor origin to the website, but I don't stop there. We track every aspect of the effort to determine which elements of a website are most productive. If traditional media is tested in some markets and not in others, we measure and compare results as well as web traffic from the various test market areas. We employ website optimizer and and other analytical tools to see which website headlines, subheads, and calls-to-action are working best, as well as which links in body copy get the most action.

Enhance

As you no doubt have assumed already, the reason we track and measure is to continually enhance and refine. New or unanticipated issues may arise as a campaign unfolds, and these can result in opportunities. The competition may respond or retaliate, or new technology may become available. This leads back to discovery. We encourage marketers we work with to hold a weekly marketing team meeting comprised of leaders from across the organization to gauge and react to marketplace metrics. Such a team develops business scorecards containing target objectives so that progress toward those objectives can be measured and tactics implemented to push performance forward. A continuous process of improvement is the result, and that's what can put you and keep you at the head of the pack.

A Continuous Improvement Management Process

To keep the marketing team pushing forward and continuously making improvement to the marketing effort, we recommend instituting a system comprised of non-negotiable rules, scorecards, and action registers, which we will describe in detail in Part Two of this book. The system can also be used to generate continuous improvement throughout a company or organization by adding interlocking teams representing other functional areas of the business. This creates a powerful system that will enable a marketing director or CEO to fully harness the collective power of the people who make up his or her organization and keep it moving steadily forward. This system will be described in detail in future chapters.

Summary

As the Red Queen said to Alice, "Now, here, you see, it takes all the running you can do, to keep in the same place." She might as well have been speaking about doing business in the twenty-first century. Our process for getting and keeping a client on top of its game involves these six steps:

Discover
Develop
Align
Engage
Track
Enhance

Chapter Two
Discover

In the discovery process, it's important to have firmly in mind the factors that come together to create a successful marketing effort, and then go past those factors to create a brand aura that will add value beyond what the functional attributes of a product alone would command.

A basic formula many marketers will agree on is to put the "right product in the right place, at the right price, at the right time." This stops short of creating a brand franchise but it is nonetheless an essential first step. To have any hope of reaching the top of the category in which you compete, you need to create a product a particular group of people wants, make it available where those people can easily find it, and offer it for sale at a price that matches the value they feel they receive from it.

And of course, this must be done at a time they want to buy.

All that sounds simple, but in reality a lot of hard work needs to go into finding out what customers want, and into identifying where they do their shopping or in creating a website they can easily find or frequent. Beyond that, you likely will have to figure out how to produce the item at a price they see as a value, and you'll need to offer it to them at the moment they need or want it.

If you get just one of those factors wrong, disaster could be the result. You could find yourself, for example, promoting a car with amazing fuel-economy when the price of oil has just hit rock bottom, or you might inadvertently publish the Cliff Notes version of a book the day after the exam took place.

The tools we use to gather the information include internal interviews and sometimes focus groups to determine strengths and challenges, as well as the culture of our client's organization, so that we can follow that with research to determine how what our client offers relates to that being offered by the competition. We usually start with secondary research and follow that with primary research intended to reveal key insights with respect to each of the four Ps of marketing:

- Product (or Service)
- Place (where sold or how distributed)
- Price
- Promotion

So, for example, when it comes to a product or service, what does the customer want? What needs does the product have to satisfy? What features does it have to meet the needs?

Are costly features included that the customer will not actually use?

How and where will the customer use the product?

What is the most the product can cost and still provide what is desired, but still be sold at a reasonable profit?

When it comes to place, where do buyers look for your product or service?

If they look in a store, what kind of store? Is it likely to be a specialist boutique or a supermarket, or both? Do they look online? Get their information there? Does a catalogue come into play?

Will they buy it on Amazon? A specialty website?

What do your competitors do, and what can we learn from that?

How can our product be differentiated?

Concerning price, what is the value of the product or service to the buyer?

Are there established price points for products or services in this area?

Is the customer price sensitive? Will a small decrease in price result in extra market share? Will a small increase not make much difference, and so result in a higher profit margin?

What discounts should be offered to trade customers, or to other specific segments of the market?

How does the price of the product we are studying compare with that of competitive products?

Concerning promotion, where and when is the best place to communicate the marketing messages to the target market?

Will the audience be reached by advertising online, in newspapers or on TV, or radio, or billboards?

When is the best time to promote? Is there seasonality in the market? Are there any wider environmental issues that suggest or dictate the timing of your market launch, or the timing of subsequent promotions?

How do competitors promote? How should their strategies and tactics influence the promotional activity for your product?

In summary, we conduct a thorough analysis of the product or service, the customers and stakeholders, as well as its competitors, and the market or markets being served, but we do not stop there. This magnifying glass on the product and market should produce enough information to mount a successful marketing campaign, but is likely to lack what we need to create a brand image that will add worth in consumers' minds beyond the utilitarian value of what you have to sell.

What do I mean?

Well, let's consider a Chevrolet or a Toyota versus a Mercedes Benz or a Lexus of the same size. All can be depended upon to get its owner from point A to point B, but which brand will command the higher price?

You and I both know the answer. The Mercedes and Lexus brands carry more weight. But when you really examine those vehicles dispassionately, are they really all that different?

Some years ago I bought a brand new Toyota Land Cruiser. The dealership also sold the Lexus brand, and I noticed the Lexus 470 looked the same as the SUV I was buying except for some chrome and the Lexus brand markings.

So I asked my salesman, who was writing up the sale, "What's the difference?"

"A tilting steering wheel and $6,000," he said.

Know what? He was wrong. As I was driving away from the lot, I noticed that my new Toyota Land Cruiser also had a titling steering wheel.

So there you go: Two cars, identical except for some chrome. What did the manufacturer do to get $6,000 more for one of them?

He created a brand image.

How do you create a brand image?

One way I have found is to tell the brand or company's story. You see, every person, every company, every brand has a story, and telling that story can create a bond with potential customers.

Let me explain.

Having written a number of successful novels and screenplays, I can say with some authority that aside from the particulars of place and time—in other words, when the temporal aspects or veneer of a story are removed—almost all successful tales boil down to the same basic plot. Here's the essence of the universal story:

As in the case of Jack and the story of the beanstalk, or Dorothy and the Wizard of Oz, a sympathetic character—the hero—ventures from his or her everyday, "ordinary" world into a place or region unlike any he or she has ever known. There, forces are encountered that attempt to destroy the hero, but the hero perseveres. He or she pushes forward in what may seem a lost cause. Yet unseen hands—call it Grace or Providence if you will—come to his or her aid, and after a great struggle and a dark moment when all seems lost, a decisive victory is won. The hero then returns home in possession of the elixir. Usually this takes the form of knowledge or newly acquired understanding that translates into power or opportunity the hero can share with the people of his community. In classic fairy tales the Cinderella character gets the prince, or the once ordinary young man wins the daughter of the king, and the two of them eventually become king and queen of the land and live happily ever after.

This story—often called the "hero's adventure"—creates a bond between the reader or viewer and the protagonist (your brand) because it is the story of each one of us. When you think about it, life itself is a series of "hero's adventures," one after the other. We all face challenges that must be dealt with and overcome—challenges that take us out of our comfort zones. Think about it. When we leave home to go to school on the first day, or to college, or to our first job, we are embarking on a hero's adventure that takes us outside our ordinary world and into the unknown. Eventually, we each return home, and when we do, having faced and dealt with the challenges, we likely will find ourselves wiser and on a higher plane of understanding than when we left.

Our task, then, in addition to answering the basic questions that have to do with the four Ps, is to unearth the story of a company or brand. In the case of a company, this typically involves digging into the history, which will likely lead us back to the company's origin. We will want to find out why the founders created the company in the first place. We will want to know what caused the company to remain viable and in business up to the present day. The answers should provide a clue.

Most likely there was something unique, something special that helped bring about success. This ability is a business's *raison d'etre*. It is the basis of a story that can be the springboard to greatness. Time and again we have found the path to success starts that way. It's what sets a company apart and gives it a core identity. When that identity is known, recognized front and center and practiced day in and day out by the leadership and staff of an organization, a powerful signal is sent to the world outside.

Here are some questions we typically ask to get at a company's story:

1. How did the company come to be in the first place?
2. Why do people like to work here?
3. When someone outside hears the organization's name mentioned, what do you suppose comes to mind?
4. What does this organization do better than any other?
5. If the organization were to cease to exist, what would be lost as a result?
6. Looking forward, what does leadership of the business wish to achieve?
7. What is the image or reputation today?
8. What do people like most about what they do here?
9. What would the organization be like five years from now if its leaders could wave a magic wand and make it happen?
10. What must be done for the organization to continue to exist and prosper into the future?
11. If a major story about the organization were to appear five years from now, what would its leaders like the headline to say?
12. What do the leaders believe to be the best single word to describe this organization and what it offers?

Can the company's story be summed up in a single word such as reliability? Safety? Variety? Fun? What do the answers to the question above boil down to?

That's the company's core identity? Its "One Thing?"

Try this in your own company. Stroll down a hallway and ask someone to give you a word that defines your company. You'll be fascinated by what you hear. And do not hear.

But if all you get are blank stares, take heart. A core identity exists. All organizations have their own unique story; it's just that sometimes what a company stands for and how that came about have been forgotten.

How a Client's Story Led to a Big Success

A good example of how a brand's story led to a successful marketing campaign is one for Riggs Bank, a client of mine some years ago. Changes in banking regulations soon to go into effect were to allow banks to cross state lines for the first time. In discovery we learned Riggs Bank had a long history of success, but that success had been confined to the District of Columbia since its founding in the early nineteenth century. The bank would have to expand into the Maryland and Virginia suburbs if it was to continue to prosper.

Discovery research indicated the bank was well established and well regarded in its market, the District of Columbia. It had been around a long, long time. It was regarded as safe and solid, and also stuffy and aloof, particularly by newcomers to the market and those living in the suburbs.

Digging into the bank's history, we found that Riggs had provided financing for some very special projects, including the renovation of Mount Vernon (George Washington's home), construction of the Capitol Building Dome, the Alaska Purchase, the National Zoo, the Iwo Jima War Memorial sculpted by Felix de Weldon, and the wire strung by backers of Samuel Morris from Washington to Baltimore to test the first telegraph.

In anticipation of moving into the suburbs, we recommended that the bank's image be softened in order to make Riggs more approachable and likeable. Our strategy to accomplish this was to evoke an emotion—in this case, nostalgia. Below is copy from one of the television spots and a few images from the spot on the page opposit. Imagine hearing it read by a friendly, melodious voice accompanied by soft music, with images appearing of the Capitol Dome under construction, Mount Vernon undergoing renovation, and so forth:

We've already helped put a roof on your house, and proudly lent a hand in the restoration of your father's home, we've helped you acquire land on which to build, or just enjoy, so when it's time to look for a new home, or finance an education, or simply open a checking account, give us a call. After all, we've been your bank for over a hundred and fifty years. Riggs, bankers to the most important money in the world . . . yours.

Images from the Riggs TV Spot

Then, as Riggs began opening branches in the suburbs, a series of TV spots ran that continued the nostalgia theme, calling attention to projects Riggs had been involved with in the Virginia and Maryland suburbs. Here is copy from one of those spots. As indicated by the still shots shown on the page to your left, imagine images of a telegraph wire being strung and Marines raising the Stars and Stripes on Iwo Jima:

When Samuel Morse dreamed of stretching a wire from Washington all the way to Baltimore, Riggs made the loan that made it happen. When Felix de Weldon longed to sculpt an homage to America, again Riggs lent a hand. So when Crystal Smith had a vision, she too turned to Riggs. And now, atop a ridge in Virginia, on the same foundation where an eighteenth century farmhouse once stood, stands a brand new eighteenth century farmhouse.

The result? Making Riggs the hero of its story worked. The campaign was a huge success. Riggs met all its objectives in terms of attracting new customers both in the District of Columbia and in the suburbs.

I have conducted identity studies among many leading firms and have found managers are often surprised to learn what potential for creating a power brand image exists right under their noses. Typically, a powerful belief system has endured despite growth, mergers, or acquisitions. A corporate story spawns core beliefs, and core beliefs create an identity—that identity is your brand. That's why we encourage those

Images from the Riggs TV Spot

leaders whose corporate stories we uncover to move quickly to reinforce that story and the identity it brings through indoctrination, training, communication, incentives, ratings and rewards.

Summary

In the discovery stage, research is used to find out how the history and thinking that went into the development of the product, service, or company. Moreover, we want to find out how the product relates to its competition and the target audience in terms of the four Ps of marketing: Product, Price, Place (distribution), and Promotion. But we have learned that it is important not to stop there. Creating a brand aura that forms a bond with prospective customers can be what adds value that will very likely result in an increase in profit.

One way to develop such a bond is to tell the brand or the company's story—its "hero's adventure." Most likely there was something unique, something special, some challenge that had to be overcome, that helped bring about the product or brand—something that played an important role in its success. This can form the basis of a story that establishes a bond with the target audience and thereby becomes the factor that creates value beyond the product's utilitarian worth.

Chapter Three
Develop

In the development stage, what is learned in discovery is turned into actual communications and an action plan to engage target customers. To do this, value statements are developed and written based on what was learned in discovery, and they are tested with target customers in order to determine what to say and how to say it. Often this is done in focus groups, sometimes in one on one interviews, and sometimes via electronic surveys. We seek to find what will motivate the target audience, and frequently, we are able to rank potential messages in order of importance. Our findings may lead us to modify what is said about a product and how it said, and they may prompt a client to modify the product or service so that it more fully delivers what customers want.

Factors that relate to every aspect of marketing are considered such as the attributes and importance to the target market of product features, product pricing versus the competition, how the product or service is delivered or distributed, and what avenues of promotion are likely to be effective in reaching the target market. Virtually every communications possibility is considered. When we survey customers and prospects we often learn what traditional media such as TV, radio, print they use, and even which radio stations and TV shows. We also probe to find out about the relative value of social media, podcasts, videos, blogs, and so forth to the target.

A detailed plan of action is the result.

Suffice it to say we consider how effective and efficient all forms of communications might be as we develop this plan. Nothing is overlooked. The following is a partial list:

Search Engine Optimization [SEO]
Social Media
Videos
Blogging
Webinars
Apps
Pay Per Click
Brochures
Sales Presentations
Events
Point of Purchase
Sell Sheets
Newsletters
eMail Blasts
Displays
E-Books
Printed Books
Television
Radio
Newspapers
Magazines
Outdoor
Direct Mail

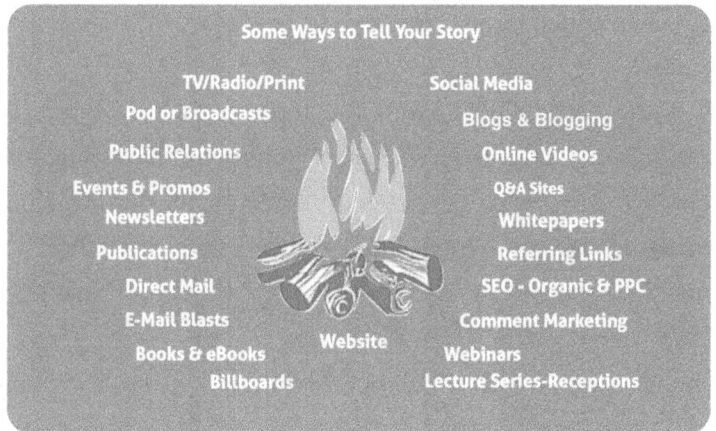

Some Ways to Tell Your Story

TV/Radio/Print
Pod or Broadcasts
Public Relations
Events & Promos
Newsletters
Publications
Direct Mail
E-Mail Blasts
Books & eBooks
Billboards

Website

Social Media
Blogs & Blogging
Online Videos
Q&A Sites
Whitepapers
Referring Links
SEO - Organic & PPC
Comment Marketing
Webinars
Lecture Series-Receptions

You'll note that we have placed SEO at the top of the above list. This is done with the certainty that step one for most people newly in the market for a product is to research that product on the Internet. As a result, search engine optimization is perhaps the most important strategy and task to be undertaken by any would-be successful marketer and ought to be a key part of the plan to be created in the development stage.

An important task will be to identify strategies and tactics to increase the brand's search engine rankings. This means identifying key word and phrase search terms and determining ways to use them that will result in attracting the maximum number of visits to the site. Suffice it to say it will be important to place the most important keywords in the content of web pages, particularly in headlines, sub-headlines, body copy, image tags, and links. But beyond this, there really is no secret formula. What is required for success is good, original content that's well written and posted frequently. That's because the people who run Google and other search engines want what their users want: informative, useful content. If that's what's provided, and done so often, a website's keyword rankings will increase.

Back in the dark ages of the Internet, oh, about fifteen years ago or so, there were a host of gimmicks SEO companies used that actually worked to fool search engines into ranking a website higher than its competitors. But those days are gone. Google, Bing and Yahoo for some time now have been able to detect artificial back links and other formerly effective schemes intended to trick them. Nowadays, using too many back links with keyword anchor text and other such tactics can actually cause harm. Google and the others can now differentiate between what's natural and what's not. Try to trick them, and you might get blackballed.

Let me say it again. Search engines are looking for sites and content that people will enjoy, find useful, and want to share with others. And they also are looking for sites that are dynamic in the sense that they are frequently updated and added to. Search engines actually keep track of that sort of thing.

Here's what we have found to be effective in moving a website from the doldrums to page one of a Google search:

Start by providing useful, up-to-date content that's a pleasure to read. You and your business may be experts in your field, but search engines don't know that unless you show them. High quality content and resources are what will get your website on page one.

Understand also that your rankings will not improve from a one-time post. You need to post a new blog or new material once a week at minimum. Three times a week is better. Why?

Google is looking for fresh, original content. And as was said above, search engines keep track.

Remember to put the keywords you expect potential customers to search in your articles and in the titles and subtitles. If, for example, you make in-bay automatic car wash equipment, as a client I once served did, and an important keyword phrase is "in-bay automatic car wash equipment manufacturer," it will make sense to write an article about what to look for when seeking an in-bay automatic car wash equipment manufacturer. Don't forget to work that phrase into the headline. This isn't rocket science. It's simply labeling your content properly.

Also don't forget to put your social media share buttons on your site. Why? Algorithms are looking for them, too, because people want to share content they find worthwhile. Making those buttons available will allow online visitors to share your website and its content with their friends and colleagues.

And here's something else. Why not give people an incentive to share? You might, for example, host a contest or product giveaway to get people sharing and maybe even tweeting your website URL.

What about inbound links? Obviously, the more inbound links you have, the more important your site must be, and thus the higher you'll rank, which suggests that it's important to look for ways to get your URL on other websites. Most magazines, news sites, as well as blogs, are looking for content. So submit some content to them. Offer to contribute an article or blog post that explains something that the news or magazine or site's readers will find helpful or useful. All this will likely be part of the SEO plan we develop.

Creating Brand Aura

Now that you have done what needs to be done to attract prospective customers to the website, what do you suppose needs to be done to turn those visits into leads and sales?

Well, bring the brand to life, of course. Create that bond.

We learned about the brand, its story and identity, in the discovery phase. In the last chapter, we saw how a brand's story, the story of Riggs Bank, was used to make Riggs a hero and to build a bond with potential customers. But suppose the brand does not have a storied history? Suppose, for example, it's a new product?

We use an approach that's been around a long time, although many in the communications business apparently don't know about it. The approach comes from Aristotle, who said that a speaker who is attempting to move people to thought or action must concern himself with pathos—their emotions. If the speaker touches only their minds, he is unlikely to move them to action. Aristotle believed, and we agree, that true motivations lie deep in the realm of passions. Let's be honest. Most of us use or manipulate facts to justify what our gut feelings [emotions] tell us we want. So, to create a brand image, emotion needs to be the payoff of the communications created for it.

How we breathe life into cold, hard facts

Think of an apple's glistening red exterior as an emotion. It's what people feel, see and react to when they choose one particular apple from the many on display in the produce section of a grocery store. Of course it doesn't occur to those

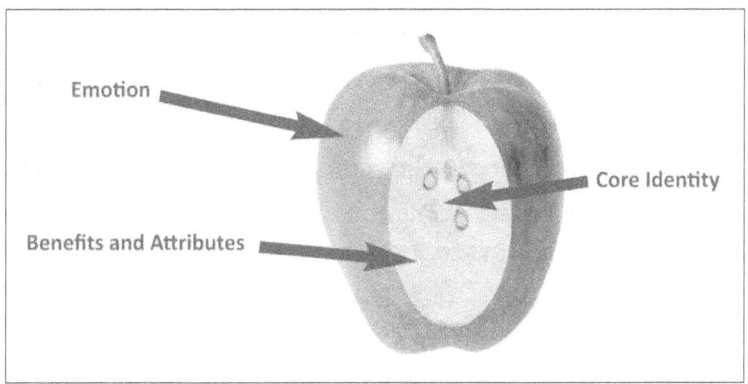

people on a conscious level, but the fruit under the skin—not the skin itself—is the real reason to eat the apple. The meat of the apple represents a product's attributes, the four Ps— the logical rather than emotional reasons to buy—its features and benefits. But just as a Mercedes will look more appealing to many prospective car buyers than a Chevrolet, particularly if priced competitively, the shiniest red apple is the one most likely to be selected.

Emotion and identity are linked in a way that gives meaning, aura, mystique and value. For example, the core identity of the Commonwealth of Virginia as a travel destination is the State's wide variety of travel attractions, including mountains, beaches, history, and theme parks. So, "variety" might be the appropriate word to use in describing Virginia's identity with respect to travel. A long list of things to do and attractions gives people a logical reason to vacation in Virginia, but we would ask, "What emotion can be attached to that?"

Years ago, a team headed by David Martin, my brother and co-founder of The Martin Agency, came up with "Love," perhaps the strongest human emotion there is next to fear.

The team reasoned that Virginia is for mountain lovers, Virginia is for beach lovers, Virginia is for history lovers, and one member of David's team had the bright idea to drop the adjectives. The rest of the team agreed, and that's how "Virginia is for Lovers" came to be.

The rest is history. Before the campaign began running, Virginia enjoyed a great deal of repeat travel business, but this loyal cohort was growing old. Only 20% of the State's visitors fell into the much sought after young family market. In three short years following the campaign launch, the figure had grown to 35%, an increase of 75%.

Emotion (love), logic (lots to do), core identity (variety) were inextricably linked. That's the underlying secret behind great and highly effective communications and what can create a compelling vision within an organization as the first step in getting everyone pulling together to bring that vision to reality.

The Creative Process

Unfortunately, great ideas like "Virginia is for Lovers" do not grow on trees. It takes hard work to get to them. We use a process to develop communications we learned from the research and development engineers at Toyota. You see, before Toyota builds cars or trucks, they build sets of possibilities to satisfy the customer's needs, arriving at a final solution by a combination of narrowing and widening. They do this by breaking the problem down into components and creating different alternatives for each. They widen by increasing the number of alternatives and the number and type of people who search for and converge on the solution.

Sounds complicated but it's really not. Here's how it works. Let's say a bicycle company is trying to design three new bike models. It can limit its creativity to three complete bikes. Or it can develop three alternative ways to make each of a bike's main components—the frame, the drive, the wheel sets, the suspensions, and the brakes. In the first case, it ends up with three bicycles; in the second, with 243 bicycle combinations. Which way do you think is more likely to develop the best new bikes?

Right, now you get the picture.

What we do next is work hard to generate a large number of ideas over a relatively short period of time. And we do not confine ourselves just to good ideas. Everything—the good, the bad and the ugly—gets scribbled onto paper and masking-taped to the wall. Where the individual ideas can be sorted in to groups of shared concepts and directions where ideas can be mixed and matched, where ways to strengthen one idea by, say, combining it with parts of another become more readily apparent, and where some of the turkeys trigger ideas that evolve into swans.

It's not confined to any set of formal processes or procedures. Like water, the creative work finds its own path to follow. And, like white water through a canyon, it flows quickly. You'd expect no less from a process based on continuous-improvement.

The Doyle Dane Bernbach revolution of the 1960s emphasized adding time to the creative process, so that the creative team would have time to give the project enough thought to make it right. Maybe so. But, paradoxically, most people in advertising, regardless of specialty, are at their best and most creative as time runs out. Give them weeks, and they'll take weeks—with relatively little to show for the time until the final day or two (see Parkinson's Law, i.e., "work expands to fill the time allowed for its completion"). As the clock runs down, the adrenaline starts to flow, and that's when miracles happen. Good teams and good creatives have shown themselves over and over to be capable of creating literally dozens of big ideas in a matter of days, not weeks. So why not start the process with days instead of weeks to go?

Here's an overview of how it works.

I typically pull together the client and a team of colleagues and explain and discuss the challenges and opportunities that have been identified in the discovery process. This includes as much factual information as possible about the brand, the audience, the competition, and the marketplace.

During this meeting, a number of preliminary ideas are discussed. Potential problems and issue are identified. The idea is to begin to get everyone on board, and to start winning client buy-in.

Then the fun begins.

After that initial client meeting, the team comes together and spends a half-day or so generating ideas. What's important here is not who develops which idea, but rather to work together, to support instead of backstab, and to develop all the ideas further.

Every idea gets written down. No idea gets criticized or mocked or discarded. Many, however, get built upon.

Then, the creative team takes all the pieces of paper on which all the ideas to date are written down, and they retreat to their own work areas. They spread the ideas out on a wall or big table. They stare at them. They talk about them. They find a compelling nugget in a confusing line. They change visuals. They mix and match.

And then the entire team comes together again. They put all the ideas up on the wall. They physically group the ideas around common themes, benefits and marketing directions. Maybe they name each direction and write out the name on a title page. They look for areas they haven't addressed. They shift some of the ideas from one group to another. Maybe they combine two or more groups that have a lot in common. Maybe they combine two or more ideas. They come up with more ideas to fill the holes they've identified. They look at ideas that aren't quite working and figure out how to help them work.

Finally, the creatives (mainly the art director) will take a day or two to lay out all the ideas as roughs—one to a page, roughly sketched or downloaded low-resolution images that simply convey the idea, all headlines in the same simple font, and so on. Just tight enough to convey the idea, but not so tight the effort wastes time and money.

And that's when the process of elimination starts, with the client decision-makers as part of the team. Together, our team and the client will go through all the ways the team could think of to meet the client objectives or fulfill the strategy. These ideas will all be in clear but rough form (often simply headlines and rough images), before too much financial or emotional investment has gone into any one approach. All the work will be there, unscreened and unedited. Together, our team and the client will compare all the ideas. We compare them to each other and to the strategy, and to what the competitors are doing. We analyze the ideas, group them, combine them, and discover parts of the strategy that the executions don't cover. We see which ones are just plain wrong, either from a factual or a marketing standpoint. Together, we discuss what makes the good ideas work and why, discarding as many concepts as possible along the way.

Sometimes the combined agency-client team will learn some new facts. Or work our way into a new strategic approach that invalidates much of the work already done. Maybe the agency will have to start over a second or third time.

No problem. It only takes another week or so to get the work on its new track. And the final campaign will be sharper and more focused—to say nothing of getting done faster and cheaper—than if a typical agency creative team had developed it in secret, the straight-line way, then sprung it on the client at the last minute.

Many ad agencies view client participation at this point as fatal, but it is vital to us and how we work. For one thing, clients have brains as well as pockets, and they just might come up with something good that no one else has thought of. Or maybe they'll tell you that you don't need that ad campaign to recruit more of a certain kind of traffic to the website because volume isn't the problem, but rather, the closing ratio is what needs to improve.

One of the most important things about this process is that clients almost always start to take a sense of ownership in the work. This sense of ownership breeds a comfort level in work they might actually reject out of hand if it were presented to them cold. This is why we often find ourselves selling our most adventurous, most unconventional, but solidly grounded concepts far more easily.

All the foregoing may sound like an oversimplification, but the process really works the way it sounds. One of the projects I applied it to was an ad campaign introducing Invensys Software Systems (ISS).

Invensys was a multinational, multibillion-dollar company that sold controls and control systems to industry. They had just merged six software companies they'd acquired (Baan, Foxboro, Wonderware, APV Systems, CAPS Logistics, and Invensys CRM) into a new division selling to mass manufacturers. The manufacturers all had factory automation. They all had e-commerce, supply-chain and customer relationship management (CRM) software. The problem was that many of these systems had been purchased at different times, at different levels of the organization chart, to achieve different objectives. Many of the systems worked at different speeds—the e-commerce software sucking in orders as fast as customers can key them in on the Internet, for example, with the automation software working at the speed of the factory's slowest machine. To make matters worse, many of the individual software systems came from different IT companies, had different architectures and spoke different languages.

ISS asked me to create an ad campaign based on how an older, slower manufacturing automation system can bottleneck fast-moving e-commerce. My team and I came up with about a dozen rough ideas in a few days.

Seeing these concepts crystallized the client's strategy—and showed them that it was wrong. The speed difference was only the tip of the iceberg. The iceberg itself was the basic incompatibility of different systems, with different functions, bought at different times by different executives to do different things at different speeds, with no ability to even talk to each other. ISS realized it could sell patches that would give disparate software systems the ability to talk to each other and work and play well together. These patches would cost customers far less than whole new systems and entail little, if any, factory downtime—but they would make ISS more money than dealing with just automation and e-commerce. So the strategy shifted to identifying the disconnect between a manufacturer's different software systems and showing how ISS could overcome it.

We sat down, and after another day or two, concepts emerged that demonstrated how the incompatibility of the software systems in many companies could gum up the works, but that Invensys could get them working together.

Three of these ideas became the final campaign. Although they were developed as one-shots, not parts of a campaign, they worked as a campaign and generated business beyond our client's expectations when the ads actually ran in *Industry Week, CIO, Chief Executive, Managing Automation,* and *Darwin*.

In all four magazines, they achieved record high readership scores. Two of the magazines liked the ads so much, they upgraded them to premium inside-cover position at no extra charge. And that record number of readers apparently liked what they saw. During the course of the campaign, ISS went from a $400 million loss to overall profitability. We're not saying that our ads were completely responsible for this turnaround. But they did get lots of prospects thinking about and talking to ISS. Here are the finished ads:

If this reminds you of the relationship between your e-business and manufacturing systems,

call us for counseling.

invensys

Summary

In the development phase, the information gathered in discovery is used to develop actual communications and a plan of action to engage prospective customers. Often, what we have learned is also used to modify or to enhance a product or service in order to elevate its appeal. Value propositions are tested and a messaging strategy developed. Vehicles are chosen to deliver the messages and a search engine optimization strategy and plan devised. Finally, emotion is employed in creating executions to deliver the brand story and thereby to create a bond between customers and the product or service we have to sell. A process is used that generates a plethora of ideas. The client is brought into the process, becomes part of it, and the result is typically that clients feel a sense of ownership in the work. This sense of ownership breeds a comfort level in work they might actually reject out of hand if it were presented to them cold.

Chapter Four
Align

Having found out what customers really want and perhaps having modified a product or service accordingly, it is quite possible effort will be required to insure the organization will deliver on the brand promise and positioning identified in the development stage. In addition, the website may need work and modifications may need to be made to packaging, perhaps decor in the case of retail outfits, and to the product itself, or to pricing. New or alternative methods of delivering the product or service to customers may make sense.

Training, or at minimum orientation of employees may also be necessary. After all, an organization thrives when its people really know their brand, believe in and live it. But often we have found that more than training or orientation needs to happen if a company is going to be able to rise to the top of its field and stay there. In such cases, the discovery process has turned up major structural issues. Maybe as a result, I have recommended that the way the business operates needs to be altered so that when a problem develops, employees closest to it can act quickly to extinguish what might otherwise turn into a raging, three-alarm fire. That could certainly be the case if employees down the line are forced to wait for someone at headquarters to be informed, brought up to speed, and then to make a decision concerning the proper course of action.

This raises an important question. How can a business best make the sort of major structural change that may be required?

How to Institute Major Change

In the past twenty years, we have noticed that companies around the world are finding that in our fast-moving global economy, the old way of managing through "command and control" just doesn't cut it. The top guy and his surrogates simply cannot be everywhere at once. Employees and workers down the line need to be empowered to make decisions on the spot and to keep things moving forward. For most businesses this means organizing into empowered, interlocking teams.

How can this kind of wholesale change be implemented?

At least two methods exist for implementing major change. The common approach is called the "define and convince" model, in which an assigned expert (or expert team) defines the change specifics and convinces the rest of the organization to follow its blueprint. This model works best in small companies, largely because of the close link between the company's leadership and its workers. But in large companies, the process is slow, seldom wins widespread buy-in, and often requires extensive infrastructure and procedural controls to maintain the change.

The other method is the "participative model." The leader defines change goals and challenges the work force to define and execute the changes. The actual process involves a series of facilitated large-group sessions for convergence and decision-making, positioned around smaller group activities. This is where the testing and learning takes place. This approach works best because rapid assimilation of knowledge and buy-in usually takes place across the organization. Nevertheless, old-line managers often hesitate to use it because it requires the leaders to trust workers with the details, instead of those whom they perceive as experts.

Participative change roles are quite different from those in the design-and-convince approach. Leaders are not order givers, but participants in learning and decision-making. Experts do not define specific changes, but rather, they provide substantive knowledge. Workers are not "change targets," but full participants in learning and decision-making.

Even though it is rarely used, participative change is not new. We won't go into extensive detail as there are several books on the subject including *Whole Scale Change* by Dannemiller Tyson Associates and *Large Group Interventions: Engaging the Whole System for Rapid Change* by Barbara Bunker and Billie Alban. These books propose many tools and techniques for engaging the work force. Often they are different in style, but both are based on the idea that the work force should be engaged and involved. Be aware that the approach may benefit from special facilitation skills for orchestrating the large group sessions. Plus, an organization's leader ought to understand the process and have the confidence to empower the work force.

To make change happen, leaders need to set targets and make strategic decisions. The people who have to live with the details make up the group that ought to determine the details. Administrators are not needed to control the process or define the results. To make sure change happens in a timely fashion, milestones ought to be set that will mark key points of system integration. These large group sessions are forums for defining what needs to be done and who need to do it, and for making decisions on major integration issues.

System integration points are milestones at which the forced narrowing of possibilities takes place. Directional decisions might be made prior to the large integration meetings in change-agent cross-functional team meetings to winnow down the options. These decisions will be reviewed and the rationale explained at the larger meeting. But to assure buy in, final decisions selected from viable options should be left to the larger group. For this reason, milestone events should be attended by virtually everyone in the company who will be impacted by the change and the new procedures. The more who take part, the better. This is how ownership is achieved. Also, large sessions make the progress highly visible and provide opportunities for visible support by upper management. This is important to maintaining momentum.

Scorecards

In Part Two of this book, a management system will be explained that can be employed to insure the company is constantly working to improve and upgrade the marketing effort. The system can be used to implement continuous improvement in other functional areas of the business as well if management so desires. Business scorecards are part of this system and deserve a mention here.

The reason scorecards are needed is that change for the better typically has to take place incrementally. It's almost always unrealistic to think an organization can go from good to great in a single step. Business scorecards are an integral component of our system because they are repositories of an organization's goals—the key destination points on the corporate journey to greatness. An important feature of scorecards is that they can be brought together from each area of an organization to form a picture of what is going on throughout the business at any point in time. Having this picture in focus helps leaders make the critical and timely decisions needed for success.

Focusing on more than one or two areas of the business will be required if company-wide improvement is the goal. The task might be compared to that of a Little League baseball coach who is trying to build a better team. He needs to do what he can to improve every aspect of the game he possibly can—the pitching, hitting and fielding of the young players who make up his team. To overlook any one of these three major areas could be what brings about a losing season.

Each business area has a number of activities that affect its overall performance—just as in baseball. Under hitting, for example, there would be different things to work on such as hitting curve balls, fastballs and change up pitches. Fielding would, among other things, include handling ground balls, flies, throws from the outfield to the cutoff man, and throwing the ball from third to first base.

Each player has different metrics he needs to work on, depending on his position. The catcher has to worry about getting the ball from home to second on a steal. The short stop has to think about handling a short hop and the accuracy and speed of his throw to first. All these activities combine to produce a winning or a losing team based on how well they are performed. It is the same in a business organization.

Everyone involved in the discovery stage of our engagement with a client will look for areas of the client's business that could be improved. If possible, a metric will be established as a target to shoot for. Obviously, the target needs to be realistic, and frequently our client's organization will be far from where we would like it to be. If, for example, world class is 99 percent and the client is at 75 percent, it would not make sense to set the goal at 99, knowing we will not be able to reach that goal for more than a year. A glide path needs to be established by setting milestones. Perhaps the goal for the first three months might be to move from 75 to 80. Once reached, the goal might be to move from 80 to 85 and so forth. Goals need to be achievable while moving the organization in the right direction.

Summary

Having identified in discovery what should be done and having created a plan of action and specific communications in the development stage, certain aspects of the brand or company may need to be brought into line so that the brand delivers fully on the promise to be communicated. As the old saying goes, "Nothing will kill a bad product faster than good advertising." How so? The advertising will persuade people to try the product, and once they do, if it doesn't perform up to expectations, they will never buy it again. Alignment may involve everything from modifications to the product itself, to training or orientation of employees, to a wholesale change in how the organization operates. There are methodologies for accomplishing such change. Moreover, it may not be possible to reach every goal right out of the box. Some may take time. This is when business scorecards may come in handy in that they can be used to establish milestones and to monitor progress toward what at the outset may be a lofty goal.

Chapter Five
Engage & Track

Once alignment has taken place, the time has come to go to market. That means rolling out the communications and engagement plan. This may involve a blitz by the sales force, heightened social media activity, advertising on the Internet, events, promotions, and traditional media—whatever the plan calls for.

Engagement is where many marketers and particularly marketing agencies begin and end what they do. They think they've done their job just as the executives at Warner Communication thought they had done their job when they bought Atari for $28 million. History showed they were wrong. They needed to continue pushing to get better and better. As has been said, in today's world if you are standing still, treading water, you are most likely losing ground to a competitor somewhere that's hungry to take away your share of market. That's why tracking is so important.

We Track Everything That Can Be Tracked

We pay close attention to what works. For example, are Google search rankings increasing? What is delivering the most leads, where are they coming from, and are those leads turning into sales? Is our message getting across and is how prospective customers view the product changing in a positive way?

How do we find the answer to that last question?

Many clients have compiled email lists. If a client isn't collecting emails, we will typically recommend implementing a program to do so—newsletters and giveaways, for example, are excellent ways to collect opt-in email addresses. Such a list can be invaluable because it can be used periodically to electronically survey attitudes, likes and dislikes toward a company or its products.

But how customer prospects view the effort and whether or not our client's message is getting through isn't all we want to know. With respect to the website, for example, we can measure which headlines and sub-headlines, and which calls-to-action are working best, as well as what links in body copy are getting the most action.

We often test copy to see what elements of a website are most productive. Winning headlines can be determined by using A-B testing to see which drive the most conversions. This is accomplished by employing A-B testing tools that measures what users remember, as well as what they like the most or least about the designs and mockups a website contains.

We put Google Analytics to work to track visitor volume and where visitors are coming from. Let's say for example we test traditional media in a particular geographical area. We can use Google Analytics to see what sort of boost, if any, we get in the number and quality of inquiries from that area.

For a number of years when I was back at The Martin Agency, I was in charge of a project that involved hundreds of thousands of interviews that tracked awareness of clients' advertising. Eventually, we were able to construct a mathematical model for participating clients that correlated advertising exposure and the brand awareness generated. As you will see, we eventually were able to relate that awareness to the sales achieved. Our goal was to find what amount of advertising exposure produced sales at maximum efficiency.

Over time we were could see a direct link between unaided recall and product sales. We found that this linkage for transaction-oriented products existsed when a competitive point of difference, viewed as a benefit, was getting across to the target audience.

In that study, which continued for a number of years, unaided recall was compared week by week with actual sales. The products we studied ranged from packaged goods to whiskey to agricultural chemical sales to theme park visitation. Our primary task was to determine precisely how much advertising weight was required to bring awareness to the desired levels. What we learned enabled us to adjust our media spend to the optimum level. In other words, we were able to tell clients what return they could expect from a particular media plan. The plan that delivered the highest profit was the one to run with.

Usually, advertising builds on a base of awareness. Past efforts are a springboard, which is one reason maintaining a consistent brand aura or personality is important. Inconsistency can actually cause harm. We saw that awareness would change weekly as a campaign unfolded and that advertising executions that were inconsistent or in no way related to those that had gone before failed to move the needle. In fact, awareness often declined, meaning they were a complete waste of money.

Since we tracked product sales and advertising over a long period of time, we eventually were able to predict what sales would occur based on how many target rating points (TRPs), which are a measure of ad exposure against target customers, were run over a given period of time. This allowed us to calculate the TRPs needed to push awareness to an optimum level. All media, including broadcast and print, were reduced to TRPs for this exercise.

To put the question we wanted answered simply, we wanted to know how much advertising had to be purchased to achieve the awareness needed to generate a given level of sales. That may sound logical. You buy media exposure to make people aware of what you have to sell and of the benefits offered. Some will buy. So why do we need a media model?

The reason is that people forget. They remember with repeated exposure and forget with the passing of time. Also, the rates at which people remember and forget vary, depending on such factors as competitive advertising activity, availability of the product, and the inherent interest in what is being sold. The model we developed took all this into account. It allowed both learning and forgetting to occur during the same week. The formula is:

$$A = bX + cY$$

"A" equals the amount of unaided advertising awareness at the end of the week, "X" equals the number of TRPs run during the week, and "Y" equals the percentage of unaided awareness at the beginning of the week; "b" is the learning coefficient, "c" is the retention coefficient. These variable factors are identified through an awareness tracking study for the particular brand. Once the learning and retention coefficients were known, together with the relationship of unaided advertising to sales, a media schedule could be developed to generate the awareness necessary to produce the sales forecast.

The reason for all this tracking and measuring is of course to continually enhance and refine what we do, which is the topic of the next chapter and, in fact, the rest of this book.

Summary

Nowadays tools are available to measure just about everything to do with a marketing effort, from awareness and attitudes to website visitation and lead generation, to which headlines and subheads do the best job. Obviously, we want to do more of what's working and to eliminate what isn't, and our tracking effort should be designed for that purpose. Eventually, if you do enough tracking and record keeping, you may be able to construct a mathematical model, as we did for participating clients at The Martin Agency, to determine what level of activity, and therefore what amount of spend, is likely to generate a predetermined level of sales. With this information, you will be able to adjust the dials until you achieve the maximum return on your investment in marketing.

"Teamwork is the ability to work together toward
a common vision. The ability to direct individual
accomplishments toward organizational objectives.
It is the fuel that allows common people
to attain uncommon results."

Andrew Carnegie [1835-1919]

Part Two
Continuous Improvement Management

Chapter Six
MM 360 Management Overview

Most of the balance of this book is dedicated to describing the management system I recommend to ensure that a business will continue indefinitely around the Discover, Develop, Align, Engage, Track, and Enhance circle so that continuous improvement of our marketing effort never stops. It's a process I began using more than twenty years ago and have improved upon and refined ever since. Some of the clients I've worked with may not be aware of it because they see only the results. How I do what I do is largely invisible to them. Others have employees who perform marketing functions, such as blogging or social media. These folks need to be actively engaged in the process because they are an integral part of the a marketing team along with me and others I may bring in. As you will see, it's important for everyone who contributes to the marketing effort to be a team member.

I will describe our management process and its benefits because you may wish to employ it as well. A top executive reading this book may even wish to use this method to run an entire company, and that is certainly possible. In fact we encourage this because we believe every business will stay healthy and grow by continually striving to improve. It makes sense that such an effort should not be limited to marketing alone. That's why we have developed a process that can easily be taken beyond marketing to include every functional area of a business or organization. In such cases, the goal is to constantly improve and upgrade in every area, and thereby to become more and more competitive.

Properly implemented, our process will put a small or a large business on a path of continuous improvement. One of my clients achieved great success using it for a business comprised of 30,000 employees in offices on every continent except Antarctica. I was proud to assist in implementing that effort.

We have found that without structure and guidance, the efforts and actions of leaders and workers within an organization can be chaotic, much as we imagine might be the case for a football team without a playbook—whose players do not know the rules of the game. Its members might work hard, may try their best, but their efforts may do very little to advance the team toward the goal because they haven't been coordinated, choreographed or channeled in a way that gets everyone doing his part to move the ball forward. That is what our process is designed to do.

The process, which I call MM 360 (for "Martin Management 360"), can be described as a methodology comprised of a few simple rules and actions involving scorecards, action registers, and interlocking teams. Once instituted, individuals will know what they need to do to succeed personally, as well as what they should do to help the organization succeed as an enterprise.

Like a playbook, MM 360 consists of activities and rules intended to result in predictable outcomes, i.e., to move a company or its marketing effort toward the accomplishment of its mission and the realization of a shared vision. Like a team that has studied its playbook and knows each play by heart, everyone in the organization works within clearly defined and commonly understood parameters. This gets the whole group working together like a championship team on a drive to the end zone.

It's Important to Establish Patterns

Managing by personality creates an inconsistent workplace. People never know what to expect. Managing by process, on the other hand, drives consistency. Influential and effective leaders are often characterized as being consistent. They have a strategy, they stay the course, and they know how to get there. They stay constant, stable and unwavering. Consistency starts with clearly communicating expectations and the consequences for failing to meet them. We call these non-negotiables.

Non-negotiables (rules) represent minimum requirements all leaders and teams throughout the company must adhere to in order to stay focused and consistent. For example, members of an organization using our method must attend certain meetings at regular intervals, they must be on time, and they must follow certain rules such as Robert's Rules of Order. Leaders should know and adhere to what team members expect of them and vice versa. Team members should know and adhere to what they expect of one another.

If you have ever been on a successful sports team, you know that everyone comes to understand what's expected of him or her and one another over time, and that no one wants to let down his teammates. Rather than wait for this to happen, each team in an organization should define behavioral expectations at the outset, i.e., what the leader expects of the team and what the team expects from the leader. Team members should also define what they expect from each other.

Team members and the leader define and document their expectations, then discuss them. Teams reach agreement on the visible behaviors defined by each expectation and commit to do their best to demonstrate them in daily operations. These are documented in a team handbook developed and written by the team. We will discuss this handbook in detail in the final chapter.

Non-negotiables are combined with specific tools such as scorecards and action registers, which we are about to explain, to create a sense of urgency and accountability. They are part of a process that gives a team and its leader to ability to identify the actions needed to move the organization toward specific goals.

A Communications System

Some reading this book will use our system to run a large company or organization. Others may use it to run the marketing effort, and others will use it to run a small business of less than a dozen employees. Communication will not be a big issue for marketing or a small business, but it's an ever-present challenge in an organization made up of hundreds or even thousands of people. Our method provides a way for the leadership of a large organization to communicate quickly and effectively and to coordinate efforts and activities of teams up, down and throughout the business.

This is possible because the organization's teams interlock so that communication can flow freely from one team to another. Many individuals will be on a team they lead, and they will be members of a team on the next level up.

For example, the head of manufacturing at an industrial plant might be the leader of a team made up of the leaders of each production line team. But he or she will also be a member of the primary team headed by the plant manager—along with peer team leaders from engineering, marketing, material supply, and other disciplines that operate from the plant. In this way, what happens or is decided in a primary team meeting can flow quickly to the manufacturing group and to the other areas of the business through the team leaders of each.

Any number of teams can exist within an organization, starting with the primary team, which is headed by the top leader in the business and his or her direct reports. The team structure then cascades throughout the organization at all levels and functions.

Business Scorecards

Business scorecards were touched on in the alignment chapter and will be discussed in depth in a future chapter because they are a key component of the system. They represent a simple and concise tracking mechanism that allows a team to monitor and respond to business metrics. The purpose of scorecards is to provide a clear and concise business

Business Scorecard									
Key Business Focus Area	SMART Objective	Target	Owner	Tracking Frequency Visible Indicator					Comments
				8/3	8/10	8/17	8/24	8/31	

focus for each team and to drive the direct lines of accountability for each team's contribution to the overall effort.

When MM 360 is used to institute continuous improvement throughout the entire company, the primary leadership team—the CEO or COO and his or her reports—takes on the task of developing a global scorecard to measure the overall performance of the organization. The global scorecard should address each important area of the business. Objectives should be high-level and supported by objectives incorporated on scorecards at other levels of the organization. This is how the leadership team is able to get everyone and everything moving toward accomplishing the organization's performance goals.

Once the global scorecard is complete, teams down the line should begin developing scorecards specifically defining how they support the global scorecard. Each team should have a minimum of one objective for each key business-focus area. Scorecard development cascades throughout all organizational levels until every team in the organization has its own set.

The primary team should review the global scorecard weekly during its team meeting. Teams in the rest of the organization should review their scorecards weekly as well, and they should review the global scorecard at least monthly.

Discussing scorecards gives meetings a sense of urgency. A scorecard also reinforces accountability. First, it does so by listing performance targets for each objective. As objectives are tracked, results are compared against these targets to gauge team performance. A scorecard also drives accountability because it identifies the owners of specific objectives. Owners track and update the metrics related to their objectives but are not necessarily the ones assigned to take corrective action when corrective action is required. Any member of the team may volunteer or be assigned to perform such a task when needed.

Teams are required to send scorecards monthly to senior management for review along with corrective action plans for any objectives not being met. It should go withour saying that knowing senior management is going to review what you have or have not accomplished is highly motivational.

Action Registers

Action registers form another important component of MM 360 management because they make accountability on the part of team members visible and measurable. It's one thing to tell someone he or she is accountable for an action. It's another for someone to know her action, or lack of action, will be seen and noted by her peers as well as upper management.

Action Register United Branding Technologies				
Action to be taken	Responsible	Deadline	Date completed	Comments

Action registers document action items that result from team meetings. An action register, for example, details corrective action plans the team and its members need to take to improve performance metrics that are not meeting targeted levels. Meetings begin with an action register review of items that should have been completed for that meeting and conclude with an action register review of new items identified during the meeting. This includes verbal and written verification of the persons responsible and the agreed upon completion dates.

In upcoming chapters we will detail the specifics of the system and its implementation.

Summary

The MM 360 management system is a combination of non-negotiables, scorecards, action registers, and when used to create continuous improvement throughout a company or organization via interlocking teams. These form a powerful process comprised of systems that will enable a marketing director or CEO to fully harness the collective power of the people who make up his or her organization.

Every member of the organization is on a team. Teams in large organizations interlock in order to facilitate communication and the coordination of efforts to support organizational goals. The primary team creates and maintains a scorecard based on the mission, goals and vision of the organization. Each team creates and maintains a scorecard with objectives that support the primary team scorecard. Every team holds a regularly scheduled meeting, preferably once each week.

Every team must create and use an action register that documents the corrective actions being taken on scorecard items that have fallen below target, as well as noting who is taking the actions as well as due dates for completion of the actions.

Chapter Seven
Scorecard Overview

Business scorecards are an integral component of our system. They are the mechanism for tracking progress toward an organization's goals—the key destination points that need to be reached on the continuous improvement journey. When used for more than the marketing effort alone, an important feature is that they can be brought together from each area of an organization to form a picture of what is going on throughout the business. Being able to access such a snapshot at any point in time helps leaders make the critical and timely decisions needed for success.

Obviously, focusing on more than one or two areas of the business will be required if company-wide continuous improvement is the goal. What's most important in your organization? Communication? A way to gauge performance fairly and accurately? Accountability? Most leaders tell us each of these is important. They find it difficult to rank them in order. That's why all three have been linked together through the scorecard.

A Balanced Approach Is Best

We find that those primary team leaders who take a balanced approach to goals and scorecards tend to achieve the best results. The top-level scorecard should focus on strategic goals. For these to be accomplished, the key is for the lower level teams to identify and focus on tactical objectives that support each strategic goal. In this way, everyone in the organization becomes engaged in support of the strategic vision and corporate mission.

Perhaps you already have a scorecard system. If so, ask yourself if it works like a thermometer or a thermostat. When someone looks at a thermostat, he or she sees the current temperature. That may be interesting, but what is more useful is one that works like a thermostat. If things are too hot, a thermostat controls air conditioning system to bring the temperature down. If the temperature is too cold, it will switch on the furnace to raise the temperature. That's how our system is designed to work.

Scorecards Help Drive Accountability

A business scorecard immediately shows employees the status of their work relative to goals, such as consumer awareness and attitudes, lead generation, website visitation, and SEO rankings. In non-marketing areas, it might encompass quality, safety, variable costs, productivity, employee retention, and customer service. When an employee looks at his team's scorecard, he should immediately know why he needs to perform because he can see how his work and the work of his team connects to the organization's goals. We suggest using scorecards that are color-coded (red for underperforming, green for on target). Anyone using MM 360 will know within five seconds of looking at a scorecard whether or not the team is winning or losing.

Scorecards Educate, Facilitate and Motivate

The scorecard should give guidance about what's important and why it is important. It should reinforce the value of winning and the consequences of losing. For example, when a scorecard is part of a system, it will help educate employees more so than one that's posted on a bulletin board where people can choose to look at it, or ignore it. People actually have to interact with a scorecard with metrics on it that relate to their area and level of the business. These are metrics they can impact, control and be held accountable for.

A scorecard should facilitate. It should start by setting the tone of the weekly team meeting. If the scorecard is updated with progress or lack of progress toward goals prior to the team meeting and is visually projected during the meeting so that everyone can see it, it will get everyone focused on what needs to be done, and who is winning and who is losing. Green items trigger recognition of accomplishments; red items trigger discussion, problem solving. Once plans are made on what needs to be done, they need to be documented in the action register with specific names and target dates for completion.

When a scorecard is linked to a way to identify who is accountable, it motivates people to get a job done. Without scorecards and action registers, leadership will have to revert to managing by personality to engage employees and cajole them to perform. In other words, management may unnecessarily have to devote more time, energy and attention to a situation the team would be addressing.

Scorecards Convert Strategy into Action

As a leader of your organization, you have no doubt spent a good deal of time and effort developing a vision and path to reach it. Scorecards can insure you are on the path, making progress because they allow the leadership team to see what is happening in each area and throughout the organization. When a company's leaders know whether income is down or up, they know how the company is doing overall. But by seeing the components of income such as quality, safety, costs, customer feedback and employee retention, leaders can tell what is happening on a deeper level. It may even help you see around corners. For example, if all the various components are improving, but the company's earnings are declining, external factors may be overwhelming the company's efforts. Conversely, if earnings are up and the various components are down, it is probably only a matter of time before earnings begin to decline.

Scorecards do not take the place of an accounting system, but they do give leaders an important tool to use to take corrective action in order to drive results. Because they enable leaders to see where particular metrics are headed, they offer warning signs that indicate action needs to be taken before green turns to red.

Scorecards can help leaders balance priorities. By establishing a few key metrics that link directly to corporate objectives, leaders can avoid metric overload and focus on those that will drive the business where they want it to go. This aligns employee behaviors with corporate objectives.

In the next chapter we will look at the specifics of developing effective scorecards.

Chapter Eight
Goals & Goal Setting

A large, family-owned business I know of ran into trouble because the owners had a habit of not sharing information with employees. After a particularly good year, the owners decided to give every employee a 13-inch flat screen television.

The Best Buy truck brought them to the loading dock, and this delivery was followed by a big Christmas lunch. The company president stood at a podium and called each employee up one by one and presented each with a TV.

Within two hours the president was beside himself with anger and frustration.

Since the employees of this company had no firsthand knowledge of how the company had actually performed that year, they could only speculate based on how they personally felt. And most of them felt they had worked harder that year than they had ever worked in their lives, and all they got to show for it was a lousy 13-inch TV.

Couldn't it have at least been a 32-inch model?

What this illustrates is that in the absence of business knowledge, what is left is individual perspective, and individual perspective can be very dangerous because an entitlement mentality is often the result. When an individual operates in a vacuum, that person is likely to calculate what he believes is owed him, and the calculation may bear no relationship to reality.

This underscores the need companies and teams have to be working toward visible and tangible goals because, at the very least, this shifts peoples' focus away from themselves and on to the business of the business. As I've said and will say many times in this book, people need to know at all times whether they are winning or losing. This is what will move them away from the personal entitlement mentality so prevalent in most companies today.

Scorecards can accomplish this because they make a marketing team, or even an entire company's goals visible.

Key Focus Areas

One of the first questions to be addressed, then, is goal setting. Goals need to relate to key focus areas.

Key focus areas sometimes go by different names such as themes, buckets, and priorities. They typically cover such things as lead generation, website visitation, sales conversion rates and so forth. Beyond marketing, they may include material costs, quality, innovation, training and certification, finance, safety, productivity, and throughput efficiency.

One way to create a scorecard is to set it up using an Excel Spreadsheet. The key focus areas appear in the first column of the scorecard. The marketing team or, if the effort extends to the entire organization, each team throughout should have at least one metric that ties to each focus area. No cherry picking is allowed. The goal is to drive connectivity through common focus areas and the scorecard format, which should be the same throughout the organization. If the leader were to walk into any team throughout the organization, for example, and ask what that team is doing to support "People" or "Efficiency," for example, he should instantly get an answer.

The next column is for SMART Objectives. SMART is an acronym that stands for Specific, Measurable, Attainable, Relevant, and Timely. The team needs to help develop and agree to what they are going to measure and work toward improving. This, of course, needs to be specific to a team's role and area of the business as they relate to the key focus areas selected by the primary leadership team.

The "Target" column is used to state the thresholds of red and green, i.e., whether the team is winning or losing in the area. Some companies also use yellow and other colors to denote transitional areas. This may make sense and be helpful in mature systems, but when starting out, I recommend that only red and green be used.

The next column shows the name of the person who owns the key focus area. This individual populates the scorecard within the frequency defined as non-negotiable. One company I know of populates metrics every seven days. In this company, the owner is obligated to populate the scorecard by close of business on Friday at 5 o'clock eastern time, no matter in which time zone the owner may reside.

Ownership of Goals

The owners' names appear in the owner column. I do not recommend that groups or teams be designated as owners. It is important that owners be physically present in meetings. If a single individual is not responsible for the data and its accuracy, it will become possible to sidetrack discussion from what is going to be done about a metric that's not where it should be to whether or not the data is in fact accurate. Whether or not the owner actually gathers the data him or herself, that person needs to be able to speak to and defend it. That way, all a marketing director or company CEO has to do is look to see who is responsible. He should be able to pick up the phone or email that person to ask the status of an objective at any given moment. We suggest leaders actually do this from time to time so that every person who owns an objective will take the system seriously.

Frequency of Data Population

In a perfect world, scorecards would be updated every seven days and meetings would take place weekly. Of course, this may not always be possible. Metrics of a strategic nature, such as some that may be found at the top executive level, may only be available on a monthly basis. Even so, most teams should meet at least once a week. I recommend this because I believe it is important to build an operational rhythm that fosters a performance habit. In situations where updated metrics cannot be made available weekly, one or more persons on the team can usually predict what the numbers are likely to be. Corrective actions can then be identified and taken to head off what may be an anticipated slip in performance.

Watch Out for Unintended Consequences

In choosing metrics, leaders and teams need to be sure to consider what behavior a particular metric will drive. If only quality is being measured, for example, a factory can probably make the highest quality product of its type ever made—but it may cost a fortune. If only cost is being measured, no doubt costs can be cut, but the company may end up producing a poor quality product.

Often, metrics are selected because the persons doing the selecting want them to look good. The question must be asked, was the metric selected because it's easy to achieve? Make sure it provides useful results.

Are there too many metrics? Having too many causes confusion and too many things to focus on. Every metric does not have to be on a scorecard. Only the most important should be. If a small number of metrics are selected, they will be what the team will focus on. If a team has eight metrics, for example, it shouldn't have a problem focusing on that many each week. If the team has 25 metrics, it will probably be able to focus on ten at most. The team will probably end up focusing on those that are easiest to handle and achieve, and these may not be the most important.

The Phenomenon of Goal Creep

Even though we recommend that 15 or fewer SMART objectives be tracked by each team, I have seen that teams, particularly on higher levels of an organization, often load up scorecards with many more. This may happen due to what I call "goal creep." This takes place because those on the higher-level do not have confidence that an effective process is in place at the lower level to improve a metric. As a result, the higher-level team members may decide to track the metric themselves. This can backfire. Because the members of that team are watching the metric, it is almost certain they eventually will be tempted to take actions to improve it. Once they do, it will not be long before they own the objective.

Where Does a Metric Belong?

As was implicit in the previous discussion, it's important to identify and place the right metric at the right level of the organization. Obviously, responsibility for a metric needs to be placed where it can best be impacted and controlled. When we work with an organization and discover metrics on a scorecard that belong at lower level, we have usually found a clue that a system is not in place to link together scorecards at the various levels. It should be the job of leaders and teams on the higher levels to do this.

To determine where a metric belongs, the question to ask is whether the individuals at a level are in position to take direct action to affect the metric, or must they enlist the help of others at a different level either above or below them.

It's also important to understand that the types of metrics are different at different levels of an organization. They typically become more basic at lower levels, and of course, there must be accurate data available for a metric to be tracked. If leadership wants to track an inquiry conversion rate, for example, there must be a way to do so. If there isn't a way at present, how difficult will it be to put a system in place and is it worth it?

The journey must be worth the climb!

When Good Enough Is Enough

It's important not to let perfection stand in the way of "good enough." Often metrics can be obtained that are good enough to provide an early indicator as to whether the organization is on track to meet goals. We often see concern that the numbers available to a team are slightly off, that the team may have to wait for accounting to close the books before a totally accurate number will be available. In cases such as this, it is usually more helpful to have an early indicator than it is to have perfection. It may be possible to improve the metric's accuracy over time, but that should not stop a team or a leader from getting started.

In practice, most scorecards go through a number of iterations as time goes by. A scorecard system ought to be viewed as a living organism that can be improved upon, updated and changed as a situation or resources change.

The important thing is to move ahead. Even if a scorecard isn't perfect, putting it into practice will likely bring more and better results than waiting to have something that is. Early on, scorecards will need updating more frequently than when a system has matured.

Chapter Nine
Creating Scorecards

Assuming the entire company has opted for continuous improvement, scorecards throughout the organization should follow the same format, look the same, and the same language should communicate whether a business is winning or losing. For example, it should be possible for someone from an organization to walk into any team meeting in the building, or into that company's offices in Seattle, Miami or Montreal, look at the scorecard projected on the screen and immediately be able to read and understand it.

Cascading Scorecards

What we call the Global Scorecard is the top scorecard in an enterprise that has deployed MM 360. This could be the scorecard used by the senior management team of a global company. It could be the one used by the CMO, or by a plant manager, or perhaps by the general manager of a division of a large company. It could be the management team of a small business. Whatever the case may be, the Global Scorecard is the scorecard for the highest-level team using the process.

Supporting the Global Scorecard are Local Scorecards built by the teams that are going to use them. Everyone on a team needs to be involved and have input on this so they all buy in.

Recently, one of us was working with a company that did not do this. The vice president of operations decided to take it upon himself to develop scorecards for every team throughout the organization. After all, he told us, he had worked his way up from the bottom and knew all there was to know about each area of the business. So he took a weekend and built the global scorecard for operations, each plant manager's scorecard, every departmental manager's, and each one all the way down to the shop floor.

The goals he came up with were probably 95 percent on target with respect to what the different teams would have come up with on their own. The problem, of course, was that the teams did not own the scorecards he had built because they had not been part of the process.

Let me add that it may be all right and even desirable for management to make suggestions, and in some cases even to mandate how certain metrics such as safety or quality will be tracked. The vice president's mistake was not involving or consulting the individuals under him.

The What, Why and How of Scorecards

Non-negotiables or rules give organizations the "what" and the "why." The "what" is that each team has to have a scorecard, it has to be in a predetermined format, and it must tie to particular focus areas identified by the primary team. The answer to "why" is that everyone needs to support and be working toward accomplishing the corporate vision.

Once everyone understands what needs to be done and why, it is up to the individual teams to determine how. How will each team make the system work? For the system to work, the scorecards need to be built locally. To insure they support the Global Scorecard as intended, they need to be approved by the team at the next level up.

Setting Targets

Obviously, targets need to be realistic. As mentioned in the chapter on Alignment, if world class is 99 percent and we are now at 75 percent, it would not make sense to set the goal at 99 knowing we will not be able to reach that goal for more than a year. A glide path needs to be established by setting milestones.

Also, when starting out, we recommend all metrics be given the same weight. But as time goes by and the system evolves, it may make sense for this to change because it will likely be the case that some metrics are more important than others.

Scorecard Iterations

I've found that on average most scorecards go through six iterations before goals are identified that clearly tell a team whether it is winning or losing. This happens for several reasons. As teams work with metrics they typically learn to break them down into components that can be impacted in ways that influence the business. This is one way scorecards help to educate their users. People learn to focus on the component or components that truly drive the overall result. A scorecard needs to be revised to take advantage of what has been learned.

Sometimes a scorecard will need to be revised because individuals had pet concerns they wanted included that have turned out not to be particularly relevant. Often, though, it has to do with whether or not it's possible to obtain the data needed to track a metric. The group may come up with something they would like to know that would help monitor progress toward an objective only to find that actually mining the data simply isn't practical or feasible. For this reason, it is important to look upon developing scorecards as an ongoing, evolving process. Once a goal has been reached or is no longer relevant for whatever reason, it should no longer be necessary to track it.

Revising Goals Upward

Suppose an area stays green and never goes into the red? It will probably make sense to revise the goal by elevating it to a more ambitious level. In fact, we recommend that a metric be reviewed with such a revision in mind if it has remained green for 90 days or more. It's likely either the goal as been accomplished and should be changed or deleted, or the green threshold should be raised. This is an opportunity to motivate continuous improvement.

Scorecard Development Summary

As already discussed, the senior team sets the key focus areas based on the organization's mission and vision and develops the global scorecard. Once the global scorecard is available, each team should come together and brainstorm how it can support the key focus areas. We recommend that if at all possible each team should identify at least three objectives under each area.

Once this has been done, the scorecard should be submitted up one level for approval. This higher-level team should scrutinize each objective to confirm it will indeed support the key focus area to which it is assigned. Once this is accomplished, and the scorecard is approved, the team can begin tracking.

Once a quarter, the senior team should look at all the scorecards to make sure there are no conflicts, that specific objectives are at the right levels and that everything works together to support the overall mission. We also recommend that each team make a presentation of its scorecard and action plans to the senior team at least twice a year.

Chapter Ten
One-on-One Action Registers

Most leaders would do whatever is necessary, within reason, to place themselves in the enviable position of leading workers who possess a keen sense of personal accountability. No doubt these leaders imagine how easily tasks would get done and how quickly goals could be accomplished. They would no longer have to worry, follow up, or cajole.

We find, however, that in most organizations a majority of leaders think that day will never come. Often, they end up doing the work that others should be doing for themselves because this seems easier than lighting the fire required to compel those workers to do it. If the leaders stopped to think about it, they would realize this course of action is counterproductive. But in the heat of the moment, they often don't have time to think long term and follow the path of least resistance.

It's easy to fall into the trap of "doing for" others. A colleague of mine tells a story to illustrate just how easy. It has to do with his two sons, ages 10 and 12, who love to play sports—especially baseball.

Back when I played baseball, a player had three things: a bat, a ball, and a glove. But nowadays there's a lot more equipment—different gloves depending on the position, metal bats of different sizes and weights, wood bats, catcher's gear, and batting helmets. So our colleague bought bags to hold his boys' equipment.

Last spring, during baseball season, he would drive the boys to practice on Saturday mornings. At nine o'clock, they would be standing by the car, sipping Gatorade, and waiting. Before our friend would climb into the car, he would check the bags to make sure everything the boys might need was there.

Often it was not.

So he got in the habit of taking an inventory, seeing what was missing, which was usually half their stuff, and tearing through the house to find the errant items. Because the coach had a rule that players who were late had to run laps no mat-ter who was at fault—parents or boys, he'd have to race to the field at breakneck speed to get them there by 8:59.

One day, halfway through the season, the boys blew the horn while our colleague was searching for their gear.

The car was in the garage and the sound reverberated throughout the house. His brow furrowed, and his face flushed red. A puff of smoke exited his ears. He calmly walked to the car and told the boys in an even tone to go and find their own stuff.

Our friend realized something important that day. He had gotten into the habit of "doing for" the boys, and they had come to expect it. He had created a culture of dependency, rather than one of accountability. The responsibility for what had happened rested squarely on his shoulders, but it wasn't too late to reverse the situation.

When he and his boys got to the field, the coach stopped our colleague and said, "You and your boys are usually on time. Something unusual must have happened."

He could see the coach was about to let the boys off the hook, just as a boss might let an employee off who is usually dependable. By this time, however, our colleague had realized what he should have recalled long before. Consequences must be enforced or people will come to believe the powers that be aren't serious. He told the coach the boys needed to run.

And run they did.

Creating Accountability

It goes without saying that a sense of personal accountability is essential on the part of managers and staff if an organization is to achieve a high level of performance. Fortunately, there is a way to create a sense of personal accountability on the part of everyone. Making the person who is accountable for a given task visible for everyone to see will do it. An Action Register is the tool.

How Action Registers are used in meetings to create accountability among team members will be discussed later. But an Action Register does not have to be just a meeting tool. It can be used as well on a one-on-one basis to make people accountable outside of meetings. One company I know of, for example, had a serious problem because workers had stopped taking personal responsibility. The situation was turned around using personal Action Registers—as the following case history illustrates.

Some years ago, the CEO of a company I worked with had read a book on the topic of creating a great place to work. He decided he wanted to create a culture in which people would feel that his company, too, was a great place to work.

The CEO arranged a visit to the company's primary manufacturing facility. The factory was shut down early on the afternoon of his visit. Everyone was given a t-shirt that said the company was going to be a "GPTW" (Great Place To Work) at a company barbecue for employees and their families.

A few days following the barbecue, the CEO unveiled his plan to the company's management. This included using flip charts, which were handed out to each manager. The flip chart had a statement printed at the top that said, "What Can I Do to Make You Believe This Company Is Committed to Becoming a Great Place to Work?"

The managers were told to get their staff together once a month for a meeting at which this chart would be used. The idea was to create a dialog with workers that would lead to the delivery of the promise.

A front line supervisor at this company has a span of control of about fifty people. The supervisor would pull these people together once a month, stand before them with the flip chart and ask the question, "What can I do to make this a great place to work?"

The result was a disaster. Imagine what these workers came up with. Here is one example:

"I have lower back issues and the chair I have to sit in all day exacerbates the problem. I've done some research and found one that should help me come to believe this a great place to work, provided you get it for me. It's called the Arrow Chair, and it sells for only $1800. Here's a printout about it from the OfficeMax Web site, along with the model number."

Multiply this by fifty and you will have a glimpse of what the supervisor now had to deal with. It wasn't long before the flipchart meetings and the efforts of management to create a great place to work had resulted in a culture of dependency. Employees came to expect the managers to do their bidding, rather than vice versa. The managers were told making employees happy was part of the job. Before long, they had so much on their plates not much business was getting done.

As you might suspect, it wasn't too long before the CEO who'd had this brainstorm was gone. The question then became, "How do we turn the situation around?"

First, the monthly 'wish list' meetings were cancelled. But that alone wasn't enough. The culture of dependency continued. Leaders would arrive to work with a manageable list of what they needed to get done that day. As a manager would walk into the building, one of his employees would come up to him with a problem. To show how this would work, let's call the employee "David" and the manager "Sam."

David might say, "Uh, Sam, my paycheck was wrong this week. I worked four hours of overtime on Sunday and didn't get paid for it."

Sam was conditioned to say, "No problem, David. I'll take care of it," and one more thing would be added to his list. Because of the monster the GPTW program had created, by the time Sam arrived at his office a few yards down the hall, he was likely to have added six more items to his ever-burgeoning list. The situation seemed hopeless.

But there was a way to fix it. Accountability had to be made personal and visible. This was accomplished through the creation and use of personal action registers. Each manager was given a pad of them and instructed on their use.

The personal action register consisted of a white top sheet and a yellow second sheet that became a copy. Let's have David and Sam put on a demonstration to show how the personal action register works.

David sees Sam coming in from the parking lot. "Oh Sam, my paycheck was wrong this week. I worked four hours overtime on Sunday and didn't get paid for it."

Sam pulls out the personal action register. "Let me be sure I understand," Sam says. "You worked four hours overtime on Sunday, and when you got your check this week, it was short the amount you should have been paid for the Sunday overtime, is that correct?"

"That's right," David says.

"First, let me say I'm sorry that happened, David. It appears a mistake was made and needs to be straightened out. The person who handles payroll is Linda Johnson in accounting. She's just down the hall, third door on the right. I want you to see Linda by five o'clock, today," Sam says as he fills out the personal action register. "I'm going to circle back to you today at five to make sure you and Linda got this straight. Here's your copy of this action register. I'll keep the yellow as a record of our conversation."

In this exchange, Sam practiced active listening by repeating back to David what David had told him, and Sam legitimized the issue by telling David he was sorry it happened. Sam also got clarity about both the issue and what David needed to do about it. Sam did this by putting it in writing so there could be no dispute. If Sam had not, it is quite possible David would plead ignorance later on. Also, Sam made a commitment to David. He made it clear he would come to see him at five o'clock. It was important for David to follow up on that commitment.

When Sam sees David at five o'clock, one of two things will have happened. Either David will have seen Linda and resolved the matter, or he will not. If David did, that's the end of the story. Sam will then be able to close out the action register and file the form in Sam's personnel file.

But let's say Sam gets back to David and asks how it went, and David says, "It didn't."

"I'm sorry, what do you mean, it didn't?"

"I mean, I was in here on Sunday, put in four hours of work, and company didn't hold up its end of the bargain. It was not my error. It was the company's error, and I want my money."

Sam will then say, "Is there anything else you would like to say about this?"

"Just that I was wronged, and I want my money."

"Well, David, I am sorry you feel that way, but the path to your money is not through me. The path to your money is the one I gave you earlier. Linda is the person who can help. But since you feel as you do, I'm going to give you an extension until tomorrow at five o'clock. I'll check with you then to see if you have reconsidered. I hope you have a great evening."

At five o'clock the next day, Sam needs to see David. Of course, it's possible David may not have done anything, once again. David may be angry, but Sam should not give in. Sam needs to stick to his guns, and he needs to be backed solidly up by management above him. If David goes over Sam's head to Sam's supervisor, and Sam's supervisor sides with David, the entire action register system will crumble, fall apart, and that will be the end of it. If David continues to stonewall, the yellow sheet needs go into David's personnel file. In this way, Sam will have will begin to accumulate documentation on a problematic employee whose days at the company are likely to be numbered. The yellow sheet will be used as an exhibit Sam can produce along with others when the day arrives for David's next performance review.

Assuming they adhere to this system, Sam and his peers in management eventually will find they are using fewer and fewer personal action registers. At some point, workers will get the message. They will realize that if they go to a boss and ask the boss to do what they are able to do for themselves, the boss is going to pull out an action register pad. They are going to realize it's a waste of time to ask the boss to do what they can do themselves.

When this is understood, people will begin to do things for themselves. Teaching people to do things for themselves is to empower them. You may recall the aphorism, "Give a man a fish and you will feed him for a day, but teach a man to fish and he will feed himself for a lifetime."

Many leaders do not put this into practice because they worry about hurting the feelings of others. These leaders should ask themselves, did the man feel bad, angry or sad about having to fish for himself, rather than have a fish hand-

ed to him? He may well have felt bad or angry or disappoint-
ed at first. He may not have liked it at all until it dawned on
him he now had the knowledge and power to feed himself and
his family. The truth is feelings and empowerment often have
very little to do with one another.

Empowerment or no empowerment, some leaders will no
doubt feel uneasy about implementing this approach. They
simply do not want employees to be unhappy. Leaders want
those in their charge to feel good about the company and their
supervisors. Let me say, this is perfectly normal—most leaders
would. Nevertheless, I submit that when it comes to business,
bottom line results are what matter most. Certainly, results are
what shareholders and stakeholders at all levels of the business
expect. If the choice is between winning or having employees
feel good, winning is the right selection. Winning will benefit
everyone in the long run, including whichever employee may
happen to feel unhappy at a given moment in time.

Let me quickly add, however, that the personal action register pad is not for every company. In the case of the company just described things had become so bad there was probably no other way to turn around the situation. Whether you
decide to use this or not, you may want to ask yourself what
you are doing to make accountability personal and visible.

As indicated above, how people feel in the short run is less
important than what people do that enhances performance in
the long run. So the important and relevant question to ask is
whether the actions and activities that take place as a result of
a company's policy move the business forward. If so, the poli-

cy is good for the company and the people the company employs. The danger is that without the appropriate policy, thoughts and actions will revolve around how people feel rather than what they do, and that can kill performance. If something is not done, the organization will almost certainly fall short of achieving the level of performance it is capable of.

Chapter Eleven
Teams and Team Member Performance

Many so-called high-performance systems have come along in the past ten or twenty years such as Lean, ISO, Green Belts, Six Sigma, 5S and others. These systems were often implemented and sustained through the strong wills, personalities, and powers of persuasion of the executives in charge.

Whether or not you have been exposed to one or more of the systems, we have found that practically every business in American has exposed its managers to team training. Teams have been thought to be the key to eliminating the corporate pyramid hierarchy in order to build a more streamlined and efficient organization. Empowered teams were said to push decision making closer to the issues that need to be addressed and into the hands of those most familiar with the issues— who should presumably be able to find the best solutions. Organizing into teams, in other words, has been thought to be the way to build a high-performance organization.

Properly implemented, teams can certainly do all that. But in many cases they have not. What has been missing is that most organizations today are driven not my collective accountability but by selective engagement, and this doesn't help create effective teams.

The truth is most companies think they have teams, but in reality they do not. They have what they call teams, of course, but when the first layer of the onion is peeled away, what is exposed is a leader and his or her staff—not a team in the true sense of the word.

Let's look at an example of such a so-called team. The leader's name is Charlie. On his team is probably at least one individual who is Charlie's "go to" person. We will call him Ralph. Ralph shares the leader's values, his work ethic and belief system. The two go way back. When vacation time rolls around, Charlie will be certain not to schedule his and Ralph's vacation at the same time.

Let's think about how things work in this set up. Perhaps it has been a bad day. All kinds of issues have arisen—high absenteeism, goals were not met and several clients are upset and need attention or handholding. Just about everything that could have gone wrong did go wrong.

Charlie goes to Ralph and says, "Could you stay after work today for 30 minutes and let's brainstorm some ideas and build an action plan so that tomorrow we can get things back on track?"

What is Ralph going to say? He will say, "Yes," of course. He is ready to stay as long as necessary because that is the way Ralph is.

Then there is someone else on Charlie's so-called team. We will call him Harvey, who is the absolute opposite of Ralph. If Charlie were to go to Harvey and ask if he could stay after work, Harvey would probably say, "I'm sorry, but I have a life outside this place. I have other things to do."

Harvey is the type of employee who should be on an employee improvement plan, he should be monitored and counseled, but from Charlie's point of view, taking on Harvey's makeover is low priority. Charlie has goals to meet, clients to please and metrics he's responsible for that are going in the wrong direction and need attention. He simply has too much on his plate already.

Charlie lies awake at night worrying about Ralph. Charlie knows how important Ralph is to him, that he gives him much more than a fair share of the work to do. What if Ralph becomes fed up with all the work being piled on him, sends out his resume, gets a job offer and leaves? That would be a nightmare. Charlie would give Ralph a raise to price him out of the market if he could, but Charlie's hands are tied. Because job categories in his company have clearly defined limits and Ralph is already at the top, that action is not an option. So Charlie decides he needs to think twice before he gives Ralph more assignments. The next one could be the one too many that pushes him out the door. So Charlie comes to the conclusion the only avenue open to him is to do whatever comes up next himself.

Many managers today are in the same situation. They take the attitude, "It's easier, faster, simpler for me to do it myself."

What is wrong with this?

In the first place, it's not fair to Charlie. He already has more than he can handle. He's already close to being burned out. If he keeps taking on everything himself, he is almost certain to reach a breaking point. So what is Charlie to do? How can he build an effective team?

Building an Effective Team

It's important at the outset, or in Charlie's case if he wants to change things, for the members of a team to get together and to discuss and agree on how they will work together. For this to happen, these three questions must be answered:

What does the leader expect of the team?

What does the team expect of the leader?

What do the team members expect of each other?

The leader needs to put down on paper what he expects of the team. These should be in the form of statements about what the team members should do. For example, rather than something non-specific such as, "be available or responsive," the leader ought to put down something specific and measurable such as, "return phone calls or emails within four hours."

The leader might say, "I want my team members to tell me bad news as soon as they hear it. I don't want them to wait until the next meeting."

Team members need to put down in writing what they expect of the leader and of one another. For example, the team probably expects its members to support each other in every way—as in all for one and one for all. In other words, they probably expect each member to do his fair share of the work and not to try to shove it off on someone else.

The non-negotiable expectations decided and agreed upon should not be personality-based. They should be operational so that if a new leader comes in to run the team, he or she will be able to review the non-negotiables and pick up right where the former leader left off. Moreover, team expectations and non-negotiables should be written up, signed by all, and kept in a team handbook. When new members join the team, they need to be made aware of the expectations and be required to sign off on them as well.

Once I spoke with a Vice President of Marketing who joined a company that was using the MM 360 management model. He told us he had never in the past been able to get up to speed so quickly as he was at this organization. His team sat down with him. They showed him the scorecard, the meeting agenda and action register, and they showed him the non-negotiables that had been developed and agreed to by the leader of the team and the members of the team.

When Expectations Are Not Met

It's doubtful any Harveys would exist in a team constituted as the one we have described above. Charlie would set forth the problems confronting the team at a meeting, and if Harvey was selected to take action on one of them, his name would be placed on the action register with a due date. Surrounded by his teammates, peer pressure would likely compel him to agree to the assignment, and he would have to deliver or face them as an admitted slacker.

But suppose Harvey or another team member does fail to live up to the expectations of the team?

What should happen, for example, if an employee—Harvey—typically works only three hours a day and spends the other four hours in the break room? Obviously, Harvey is not living up to expectations, the particular one in this case being "support your team members in everything they do."

If he has built his team properly, this should not be team leader Charlie's problem. One of Harvey's team members should go to Harvey and tell him he isn't living up to the expectations of the team. By taking such long and frequent breaks, Harvey is in violation of what he agreed to when he signed on. His slothful behavior creates more work for others because they have to take up the slack that comes about as a result of his absences.

My experience has been that nine times out of ten this conversation will take care of the issue.

What should happen if a worker first goes to Charlie, the leader, about Harvey's behavior?

The leader should ask if the worker has had a conversation with Harvey. This team-member-to-team-member conversation needs to happen before any other action is taken.

Suppose the conversation is held, but Harvey continues taking long breaks?

The situation should be brought up at a team meeting, during the "around the table" agenda item. This can be done in one of two ways, depending on the maturity of the team. One would be to begin by not mentioning any names. So, if a team is new to the process, someone might say, "There is a member of our team who is working only about three hours a day and spending the rest of the time in the break room." David will now know he has now been put on notice and that the team leader is going to be looking out to see who is the guilty party.

On the other hand, in a mature team, someone might simply say, "Harvey is spending an inordinate amount of time in the break room and that's making more work for the rest of us." If this is indeed the case, others will certainly support this statement.

If the issue is not resolved once these steps have been taken and several weeks have passed, it is time for the team leader to get involved. This leads to the final topic I wish to cover in this chapter, which is individual performance management.

Performance Management

Do you dread doing performance appraisals? If you do, you are not alone. Most managers dread doing them because these managers do not have good data sources from which to draw information. the TA 360 system remedies this.

Most employees go into an appraisal with the assumption that if they have heard nothing, then they must be doing all right. Alternatively, some experience anxiety before a performance appraisal because they do not know what the appraisal is going to reflect. These situations exist because performance appraisals are typically a formal annual or semi-annual event in which the manager sits down with the employee and discusses past performance, with an eye to the future. I have found, however, that performance appraisals as stand-alone events such as this are not effective. What's effective is performance management.

Performance management is an ongoing process. The manager maintains documentation and engages in ongoing dialogue with the employee in an effort to change work behaviors and outputs. The performance management process involves rewarding and acknowledging good performance, identifying and rectifying deficient performance, and applying consequences to unchanged behavior and performance.

Our system allows leaders to collect the data necessary for continuous performance management. This is done through the meeting action register because all the actions assigned to each individual and the outcomes that came about as a result are documented there.

I have found that in a mature team, about 80 percent of actions tie to scorecard items. The action register becomes an important historical record because an analysis of who has taken actions and how each individual has performed can provide an important indicator of the contribution of each team member. In other words, information from an action register can be rolled up periodically to give a clear picture of what the various members of the team are doing to advance the business. Such an analysis can be performed as frequently as needed to provide, for example, the data Charlie needs to coach Harvey and to manage his performance.

Chapter Twelve
Creating Accountability

Is there a system or methodology in your organization to make accountability personal and visible? Does the organization delineate between responsibility and accountability? What is the role of the leader in building a team driven by collective accountability rather than selective engagement? How does the leader ensure accountability equity so the team is not unmotivated by a real or perceived disparity of engagement?

Performance is achieved when people are held accountable to act on the objectives that support the business. A key tool of the MM 360 management model that brings about visible accountability is the action register. The action register is a logical extension of the business scorecard, which in our system is constructed and deployed in a way that ensures employees focus on issues important to the success of the company. The action register brings about visible accountability and drives accountability throughout the organization. It does so by publicly documenting the assignment of tasks to specific individuals, dates for completion of tasks, and results.

When leaders implement this tool along with the business scorecard, they eliminate ignorance as an excuse for tasks not completed, and they eliminate personality from the focus of business.

Focus does not help a company a great deal unless it can be brought down to a level where that focus can stimulate and capitalize upon clear and visible, personal accountability. Let's look at systems and processes that can take an organization that is not performing up to its potential to one in which things are humming along in the direction its leaders would like it to go.

The Scorecard System

Most companies and organizations keep score. Metrics are developed, recorded and circulated, but most business people we talk with do not find them to be particularly helpful. In such cases the effort involved does not seem to be worth the benefit derived. We work hard to get the data, we run the data, build a report, and after all that energy and effort has been expended, we find we cannot really see anything that can help us improve our efficiency or way of working day-to-day.

The fundamental purpose of any scorecard system should be to tell us within five seconds of looking at it whether or not we are winning or losing.

As stated in the Goals section, a good scorecard should do three things. It should educate, facilitate and motivate. Many leaders of companies go straight to the numbers and miss what a good scorecard system should do or be. A good score-card system should be used, deployed and sustained.

A Scorecard System Should Educate

The first question to ask in evaluating a scorecard system is whether or not people understand it. Do they understand acronyms such as EBIT (Earnings Before Interest and Taxes)?

You may be surprised to learn that one of our team once

had a manager ask him what "overhead" was and how he could impact it. This was a person in charge of a large department with a good deal of overhead. To head off any potential confusion or misunderstanding, one company I know of issues a glossary of terms and an explanation of scorecards usage to new employees when they join the company. I believe this makes sense. It shows new employees what's important.

Consider this. When orienting new employees, how many companies brief them on their first day about scorecards and the metrics of the business? How many really get detailed information about what's working and what isn't?

Not many, I suspect.

If whether the business as a whole, or the marketing effort in particular is winning or losing isn't communicated to a new employee right away, what message is being sent? Unfortunately, the message may be that winning is not a priority.

The fact is people coming into an organization usually would like to know if it is profitable and how it is doing. One highly successful company I know of uses the first two hours of orientation to educate new employees on scorecards. They begin with the company's global scorecard and follow with the scorecard of the new employee's business unit or department.

A Scorecard System Should Facilitate

I believe that meetings should be enablers of the business not additions to the business. Yet a lack of meeting effectiveness typically shows up in most company surveys. This will always be the case in my view until a scorecard is used to facilitate meetings.

After a lack of meeting effectiveness surfaced as a big issue in a survey, one company I know of posted a job for fifty people to become black-belt certified meeting facilitators. Those selected were sent to a posh hotel in Scottsdale, Arizona, where they spent one month being certified. They then returned to the organization to help improve meeting facilitation across the organization.

In effect, the company built a meeting facilitation plan based on what I call the three Ps: Presence, Persuasion, and Personality. The people selected had to have presence—they had to be able to stand in front of the group and articulate and persuade them. It came down to using personality to try to fix a systemic problem. Instead of a team captain leading a meeting, an outside expert would be brought in with the effect that the team captain was no longer in charge.

Here is how meetings work at a company I believe conducts them in the right way. The meeting takes place on Monday mornings and is led by the CEO. Most attendees work in the home office and are physically present. Others who happen to work in remote locations are present via Zoom. At 9:45 a.m. in the meeting room, the company scorecard is projected on a screen and made available to those attending by computer. At just before 10 o'clock when the staff walks or tunes in, their eyes are drawn to a scorecard with about 15 items on it, perhaps three of which are red and the rest green.

Everyone knows the purpose of the meeting is not "team time." The purpose is to take care of business, i.e., to drive the business forward by identifying issues facing the company, finding solutions and making assignments to carry them out. Given that only three metrics are in the red, the participants can expect a relatively short and painless meeting.

All can also see that twelve of the fifteen metrics are green. They instantly know the company is winning.

The three red items will, of course, be discussed. No one will be allowed to leave the room until specific actions with names and deadline dates have been identified and agree to.

This is how a scorecard facilitates a meeting. It instantly shows whether or not the team is winning or losing and it pinpoints what needs to be focused upon. This becomes the primary purpose of the meeting and neither time nor energy is wasted. In the absence of a scorecard, the purpose of a meeting is likely to become individual wants and needs, and personalities are likely to become the driving force.

A System to Motivate Behavior

Scorecards will not be translated from thermometers into thermostats until a robust action register is married to the scorecard. What's important about scorecards is what is done about the data.

It's human nature that when anyone is called upon to brief a senior level executive, he or she would certainly like to have something good to say. When this is not the case, and the news is bad, most of us will invariably want to move on quickly to explain what is being done to correct the situation. But most organizations do not use scorecards for this purpose. A scorecard may show a situation is not what it should be, or what management would like it to be, but the scorecard does not show how it will be corrected.

To overcome this, some managers keep action logs or meeting minutes to document the actions to be taken that have been decided upon in a meeting. Often, however, this simply doesn't work. Those who were to take action sometimes conveniently forget their assignment or firmly object, saying that, as they look back, it wasn't clear to them they were responsible. They may add that with all the many items on their plate these days, they would not possibly have agreed to add the issue at hand— after which, to justify their inaction, they are very like to reel off a long list of the other things they had to do. This dissertation and the ensuing discussion will be a total waste of time because they have nothing to do with running the business, and the ball will not be moved forward a single inch.

Action registers eliminate this. Action Registers are married to the scorecard. It becomes a standard agenda item during which action decisions are made and recorded, including the individual who commits to take the action as well as the date it is to be completed. Everyone on a team knows the action register will be reviewed at the next meeting, and they know that if they are not going have the action completed, it is incumbent on them to negotiate a new completion date before the meeting.

Semi-Annual Management Briefings

In order to motivate, there also needs to be a scorecard reconciliation, periodically. If someone never has to brief others on performance *vis a vis* objectives, that person never really owns those objectives. On the other hand, if someone has to stand before a group and tell the story, what worked and what didn't, that person will own them. This is why I recommend that each team in an organization be compelled to brief a management team two levels up from it a minimum of twice a year and, in some cases, more frequently.

There are a couple of ways this can be done. At one company with which I am familiar, a schedule is put together so that everyone on every team knows by the second week in January the two dates when someone from the team will have to brief senior management on the team's action register. This can work, but it may also create a negative behavioral consequence. It's human nature for the team to want to make the briefing as positive as possible. As a result, a good deal of activity may go on behind the scenes to make things look good at the times the briefings have been scheduled.

Perhaps a better and potentially more effective way is the approach taken by another company. In this organization, each team is made aware someone from the team will be required to brief senior management twice during the year, but they are not told the dates these briefings will occur. All they know is that on any given date on which they are having a meeting, the team leader may get a call letting him or her know senior management will be joining them that day. This should not be a problem for the team or its leader if they have established a meeting rhythm and things are moving along as they should. The people we know who work this way like having senior management sit in because it gives them the opportunity to ask for additional resources when needed.

Scorecard Reconciliation

As has been discussed, it's important that scorecards throughout the organization relate to and support each other. To insure this, it makes sense for senior management to take a careful look at all scorecards throughout the organization at least quarterly. All scorecards should be printed out and laid side by side for a close look. This will serve several purposes. It will mitigate the possible gaming of the system, and it will make sure the scorecards link to and support one another. This exercise will also provide an opportunity to judge whether objectives and accompanying metrics are at the right level.

An example of how they can end up on the wrong level was given under the heading "Goal Creep" earlier in this book. Suffice it to say questions should be asked. For example, if a team is not achieving a goal in one area, is there another team somewhere that could be supporting that goal? Scorecards should not be allowed to become independent reporting system silos.

Chapter Thirteen
Action Register Non-Negotiables

When a SMART objective measurement is not where it needs to be, the meeting action register is used to record and document the action remedy decided upon. This includes who has agreed to be responsible for taking the action and the date agreed upon for the action to be completed.

Ample time, usually the longest allotted to a single agenda item, should be spent at the end of each meeting to review agreed upon actions and for those who are to take the actions to acknowledge that they accept the assignments. In other words, what each action will consist of should be made crystal clear, and the persons accepting the assignments should clearly confirm they understand and agree to the assignment. In addition, specific dates need to be identified and recorded. In no case should they be left open to interpretation such as "TBD" or "ASAP"—even if it's not clear how long an action will take. Having a date sets a process in motion because a method should also be in place and understood by all for renegotiating action due dates if for any reason they cannot be met.

When such non-negotiable rules are in place, action registers become a vital component of an effective accountability system. Let's take a closer look.

When Due Dates Cannot Be Met

An action and the timeframe for its completion may have made sense at the time it was agreed upon. The person who agreed to carry it out may have believed he or she would be able to do what was called for without a problem. But things change, and sometimes a task is not what it at first appeared to be. Perhaps, the action isn't as easy to accomplish as he or she thought, or for some reason it cannot be completed in the time allowed.

What should happen, then? Let's look at the leadership team of a company that uses this system.

The team meets on Monday mornings at ten o'clock. An action register review is an important agenda item for this team. If someone is supposed to have an action completed but cannot, a non-negotiable rule is that the individual must renegotiate a new due date with the team leader by the close of business Friday. This brings about a couple of desirable results. For one, it causes people to look at the action register before the day of the meeting.

Let's say Sam is supposed to have something done by the meeting on Monday, but cannot. So, he goes to the team leader on Friday and explains the situation. The leader is likely to be gracious about it and to agree to a new due date because Sam has thought ahead, taken responsibility, and behaved in the way the team leader expects of his team members. But, what if Sam does not go to the leader on Friday?

When Sam starts making excuses in the meeting, the leader will show his displeasure. He might say, "Sam, I don't recall having a conversation with you about the fact you weren't going to have this done. You and I need to have a follow up conversation about this issue later. You need to explain to me what isn't clear to you about the meaning of the words non-negotiable. Now, let's move on."

The leader has taken an important action. If he or she does not say something like this and have the follow up meeting with Sam, she can expect as many as half the team to fail to have actions completed at next week's meeting. Not only does the leader need to be clear about this, the process for renegotiating a due date also needs to be clear. Doing so with an email should not be an option. A conversation either in person, by computer or by telephone must take place and the leader must affirm the new due date. This means the owner of a pending action for which the due date needs to be renegotiated should not wait until Friday afternoon to begin trying to get in touch with the leader.

When it becomes clear to everyone that non-negotiables are just that, that rules are rules and action registers are serious business, meetings will begin to move along quickly. They will cease to be drawn out affairs because the focus will be on the business and the related actions needed or taken. A person will give his or her report, and attention will move to the next agenda item. Extraneous discussion will not be necessary. If a scorecard meeting is run right and contains a manageable number of red metrics, it should only last anywhere from 45 minutes to an hour.

Who Should Keep the Action Register

Every team needs to have a person assigned who keeps the action register in meetings. This role can rotate, but the role itself must be a dedicated one, and it should be performed in real time. This means the actions, persons responsible, and due dates should be recorded on the action register in the team meeting at the time they are decided upon. Ideally, the action register will be projected on a screen so that no mistake can be made about what is being recorded.

It is also important that only one centralized and universally accessible action register exist—either a hard copy in the team handbook or electronically in the handbook on a server—and that this be kept current at all times. An action register is an important way to create visibility so anyone who needs the information should have access to it at all times. Software tools are available for this, or a linked Excel spreadsheet can be used. When a due date is renegotiated, for example, the one who renegotiated the date should go into the system, change the date in the comments section and note who agreed to the change and when.

Unless a centralized action register exists, inconsistent records will most certainly come about and leaders and others will not have access to the most current information.

Accountability Analysis

Periodically, information from an action register can be rolled up to give a clear picture of what the various members of the team are doing to advance the business. Such an analysis might be performed quarterly, using the centralized action register database. As perviously stated, for a mature team, about 80 percent of actions tie to scorecard items, which is to say this analysis is an important indicator of the contribution of each team member.

Chapter Fourteen
Communicating with Everyone Involved

If the marketing team is small enough, all necessary communications can take place at the weekly meeting. But if the marketing organization is large, such as would be the case with a multinational firm, or if for example the continuous improvement effort is company wide or includes several functional areas, a system will need to be in place to communicate with everyone so that they will be on the same page and pulling together.

Is a communications system in place to drive a sense of urgency? Is there a cascading waterfall, or a battle rhythm of communication, that replicates on a regular schedule? Has the organization become dependent on technology to drive communication?

The most effective communication is a two-way street. I have seen that in top performing organizations, communication is not a random event, but rather, it is a planned process—just as is the case with any other business function. When planning a communication strategy, it is important to incorporate key elements that bring focus to meetings rather than endless discussion, enable participation, and provide a consistent flow of information.

Frequency: Since meetings tend to be the primary two-way communication vehicle in most organizations, a minimum frequency should be established for meetings of particular groups based on business cycles and needs. A team should meet at this minimum frequency to ensure timely communication with its members.

Purpose: It's important to define in advance the business purpose and outcomes desired from a particular meeting. Specifying the purpose and outcomes enables focused preparation and clarity around topics, and it defines the level of urgency for activities that result from the meeting.

An Agenda: Every meeting ought to be planned around a standard agenda, which not only lists the topics to be discussed, but also the time frames in which to discuss them and the person who will lead a discussion or give a presentation. A structured agenda reinforces the business focus and sense of urgency for communication and action relative to the business topics. The agenda ought to include a status update of outstanding actions from the previous meeting as well as a verification of new actions that arise during the meeting so there is complete clarity about who is doing what and when.

Defined Roles: Meetings need a leader, a recorder and a timekeeper. These roles ought to be identified and filled prior to the meeting so that individuals come prepared to fulfill them. Filling these roles insures someone is ready to facilitate the agenda, document actions, capture information and document decisions.

Rules: There ought to be ground rules that define acceptable and unacceptable behavior in meetings. Some examples: no interruptions, be on time, respect one another, stay on the topic, everyone participates and cell phones off.

An Audit Process: A process should be in place that monitors and provides a basis for improving communication. One way is simply to ask the end of each meeting, "What went well during this meeting?" and "What needs to be done to improve the next meeting?"

It's important to keep in mind that communication only occurs face-to-face. Any other communication is advertising. Advertising can reinforce and supplement face-to-face communication but it should never be expected to replace it.

Clarity System

We have talked about scorecards, and we have talked about action registers. How does it all fit together? How is a battle rhythm created? The communications system is the key. It must be built and implemented based on how the process needs to be replicated. To illustrate this, let's return to a meeting of the leadership team that meets on Monday at ten o'clock.

When the team walked into the meeting, the scorecard was on the screen. Then, a meeting agenda is put up. The first item is the Action Register review.

How long should this review take?

Only those items due on that day need to be reviewed. If an item that was due is not completed, it should have been renegotiated. So the time spent on this item should be short.

Next the Scorecard is on the list. Unless items have been green for 90 days or more, only red items and potential solutions will be discussed. The actions to be taken will be captured and recorded under the agenda item, Action Register Review.

This brings the meeting to "Around the Table." This should not lead to a dissertation on the part of each individual of what they do each week. Rather, it should be a 30 to 60 second opportunity to bring up an issue and get it on the action register, or to call attention to something the group needs to be aware of such as the pending visit of an important customer.

Recognition is next. A company will almost always benefit from institutionalizing recognition as a weekly discussion point. Some are uncomfortable with this because it seems to them to be forced. Even so, we suggest putting it on the agenda as a non-negotiable item because if recognition is not institutionalized, my experience has been that it probably won't happen.

Let's take a look at how this might work. The agenda at our example company cascades throughout the organization. Each member of the leadership team heads up his or her own team that meets weekly. Members of these teams head their own teams, and so on throughout the company. This enables recognition at the lowest level team to be passed up from team to team until it reaches the very top. When the top team reaches this item on the agenda, the person assigned to coordinate recognition gives his or her report.

The person might say, "This week we had eight recognitions that came up to us. Here they are. Hannah on the third shift at our plant in Walla Walla did such and such, John in Peoria did so and so . . . " and so on.

Each recognition is then given out to a senior executive in the room to follow up. Over the next seven days, these senior executives will make contact with the person they were assigned. If the she will be in the office or plant where the person works, she will visit that person and speak to him personally.

If a face-to-face visit isn't possible, she might call the individual on the telephone and say something such as, "Hello Gloria, this is Hillary Starling, VP of Sales. I want you to know that we talked about what you did for the company at our executive committee meeting earlier this week. We want you to know that your action was spot on, and we sincerely appreciate your quick thinking. . . ."

The leaders of this company are making visible actions that benefit the company in a way that can literally transform behavior throughout the organization—literally lift it to a new and higher level. I submit that if a mechanism to make this happen is not in place, it will happen only sporadically or not at all.

Pass Up, Pass Down

As has been discussed, there is a big difference between one-way communication and two-way communication. Many organizations have mastered one-way only. Because of this, the leaders of these organizations have falsely convinced themselves they are communicating when they are not communicating.

Anyone who has a teenager in the house or has been a teenager not so long ago will understand why this is so. When one reaches the age of sixteen, gets a driver's license and wants to start going out with friends, most parents will give that young person a curfew. So think back. When your mom and dad gave you a curfew, did they write it on a note, side it under your bedroom door and say, "Honey, when you get a chance, give us some feedback."

I doubt it.

Usually, people tell us this message was delivered face to face, and it was not delivered only once. When many of us left the house, one of our parents would say, "When will you be home?" This wasn't really a question. The parent was seeking validation that the message had been given and received.

Why was this important?

Once that verbal affirmation occurred, the teenager could be held accountable.

Newsletters, bulletin boards, emails blasts and the like are much like sliding a note under a teenager's bedroom door. They do not require people to engage. But suppose they do get the message? If what we are attempting to communicate is not to their liking, such as an 11 p.m. curfew, they may feign ignorance.

The pass up, pass down system can be beneficial in big ways and small. Once, one of our team members got a call from a friend at another company who said people in suits were walking around in the building where he worked. Naturally, the friend wondered if his company was being sold. The rumor mill was already in high gear. It turned out that the people in suits were from a company that had just become a new customer and were on an orientation tour. The rumors could easily have been avoided if the fact that the tour was going to take place had been brought up as a pass up, pass down agenda item.

Another company I know of with about 8000 employees changed its health care package. What had been a generous package became less generous. Historically, this company had communicated a change in benefits through a letter and an information packet sent to employees' homes, and of course, the information was also posted on bulletin boards throughout the company. This time, however, leadership decided to do it differently because they now had a past-down process in place. This was possible because everyone in the company was on a team and each came together once a week in a meeting. It started with the top leadership team in the company, which met on Monday mornings at 10 o'clock.

This company's pass down process used bullet points, which are the key points leadership wants everyone to know during a communications cycle. The pass down is agreed upon in the leadership team's Monday morning meeting.

This particular pass down went something like this:

Our health care benefits are changing. We are going from Company A to Complany B. We are going from a co-pay of $20 to a co-pay of $40. We are going from a family deductible of $100 to $1000.

These points were approved in the 10 a.m. Monday morning meeting. At one o'clock on Monday, the vice presidents had their team meetings and verbally delivered the pass downs. At three o'clock Monday afternoon those who had met with a vice president had their meetings and verbally delivered the pass downs, and on it went until by Thursday afternoon, everyone in the company should have been informed about the change in benefits in a meeting—all of which, by the way, included a scorecard and an action register.

Sometimes the president of this company stands next to a time clock in one of the company's plants and asks questions of those punching out.

He might say, "Excuse me, can you tell me one of the pass down items in your meeting this week?"

The reply he might get could be something like, "Yes, our health care benefits are being cut. The co-pay is going to double and the deductible is going through the roof."

Although he may not like the way this employee feels, his question has validated that she got the message.

Suppose, however, he asks the question and the person has no idea what was in the pass down?

He will ask the person if the weekly scorecard meeting took place. If the person says no, the next question will be, "Who is your team leader?"

Because the leader of the company does this, people take the system seriously and it works.

The Meeting Audit

You will probably not be surprised to hear that most companies have too many meetings. The truth is many seem to be in a cycle of meetings they seem to be unable to break. No wonder we hear so many complaints about meetings—everything from those that are a total waste of time because the discussions amount to little more than gripe sessions, to those that at least accomplished something but could have lasted fifteen minutes instead of half the day—if the leader had just kept people from wandering off topic.

Meeting audits are a way to cut down on unproductive meeting time spent. I recommend that no meeting should end until everyone in attendance answers the following question: "Was this meeting an enabler of our business, or was it in addition to the business?"

The leader should go around the table and have everyone in attendance express his or her opinion in the spirit of, "If the meeting wasn't as good and productive today as it might have been, what can we do next time to make it better?"

Weekly scorecard review meetings typically should not last more than an hour. In one company I worked with, the average manager spent 23 hours a week in meetings before our system was instituted. The 23-hour figure was cut to only five once it was in place and working as intended. Two of those five hours now are typically spent in two meetings: the meeting she attends with her boss and peers and the one she leads with her subordinates. The other three hours are spent in meetings that support special projects, committees meetings, and so forth.

Cutting Down on Meetings

The MM 360 management system is meant to build a battle rhythm so that a pattern is built that moves the business forward. As this rhythm takes hold, an overall effort can be undertaken to align and streamline the company's meetings. The system should provide the basic information to run the business. Many meetings companies have are an outgrowth of not having the information they need. Meetings then spring up to deal with the lack of information. Once the system is in place and mature, it should be possible to make a list of all the meetings that take place and decide how that list can be modified and streamlined. Which meetings can be eliminated? Which can be cut from weekly to monthly or from monthly to quarterly?

Chapter Fifteen
One More Thing You'll Need

As mentioned earlier, it's important to for the members of a team to discuss and agree on how they will work together. The team leader and his or her team members will benefit by putting down on paper what they expect of each other. It's a good idea to do so in measurable terms, and everyone should sign off on this.

Earlier, a detailed three-step process was explained that can be used when a team member is not meeting expectations. First a fellow team member should have a private chat with the offender. If that does not resolve the issue, it should be brought before the entire team at a regular meeting during Around-The-Table. Finally, if these initiatives fail, the team leader will have to get involved. This and other agreed-upon procedures should be clearly stated in a team handbook.

A Team Handbook Contains:
- The Marketing or Business Action Plan
- Procedures
- Non-negotiables and team expectations
- Contact information for each team member
- An up-to-date scorecard and action register
- Historical scorecard and action register data

The team handbook is the nexus of MM 360. For a small group of marketing professionals, or a small business, this can be a three-ring binder kept in a central location. For a large organization, software can be purchased that can be used to create an electronic handbook to be kept on a central server or in the cloud. Regardless of the form it takes, a handbook should be available to anyone who needs to refer to it. Moreover, it should contain everything to do with the team and the effort the team's members are engaged in improving, including the effectiveness of marketing initiatives, agreed-upon procedures, non-negotiables and team expectations, contact information for each team member, an up-to-date scorecard and action register, and historical information and data.

The handbook gives order and consistency to the team's business by outlining its purpose and processes and serving as a public record of its work. Teams use handbooks to orient new team members and to train them in team procedures and job responsibilities, as well as to reinforce non-negotiables and to audit team processes.

Because it is available to anyone who may need to refer to it, the team handbook removes ignorance as an excuse, and it elevates expectations by holding everyone accountable. Along with action registers, a team handbook documents expectations for behavior, and it provides a mechanism for team leaders to be consistent.

Large companies using our system and cascading teams to create continuous improvement will benefit from having a fully integrated software system that ties team handbooks together throughout the organization. Such software is available off the shelf. It should be Internet based so it can be accessed from anywhere in the world via a permission-based login procedure. Moreover, different employees can be allowed different levels of access depending on their needs.

The software allows scorecards to be customized to meet the specific needs of different users and populated manually in the same manner as an Excel spreadsheet. Data can also be imported from a CSV [Comma Separated Values] file or directly from an ERP [Enterprise Resource Planning] system.

Someone with full access to the entire data base of a company, such as a CEO, can roll up information on a historical basis to determine trends, look at what is going on with a single team at any given time, past or present, or slice and dice the data in a myriad of ways that will provide an abundance of information he or she can use to run the business. For example, the leader can quickly review scorecards from each team. Because progress toward SMART Objectives is color-coded in such systems, how each team is performing can be seen at a glance. Past and present data is there, so trends can be spotted easily. Action registers are linked to each scorecard, so the leader can see what corrective action plans are in place and being implemented, as well as when a resolution is due. Moreover, a built-in audit system offered by the software provider allows changes to be tracked, including due dates and the personnel responsible. This makes it possible for leaders to follow up quickly on problem areas and to enable or empower those assigned to the task to get it done. It also facilitates the recognition of employees for their accomplishments.

One thing is absolutely true. The Red Queen was right. If you aren't moving forward nowadays as fast as you can, you are losing ground. Such a situation is unsustainable. The time has come to institute continuous improvement marketing at the very least, don't you agree? Better yet, why not institute it company-wide?

Use this book, or use the contact form on my website to get in touch with me: www.shmartin.com

I'll be happy to help.